ABOUT
WHOEVER

ABOUT WHOEVER

ABOUT WHOEVER

The social imprint on identity and orientation

by

KAREN SINCLAIR

Edited by Dr. Peter Jackson
Illustrated by Karen Sinclair
Cover Design by Ebook Launch

ABOUT WHOEVER

Published By Karen Sinclair
Print Edition

Library of Congress control number: 2013902766
ISBN 978-0-9814505-2-0

Cataloguing data:
Sinclair, Karen
About Whoever: The social imprint on identity and orientation
Includes bibliographical references and index

Summary: Contemporary understandings of human sexual identity and sexual
orientation are analyzed from a social science perspective.
1. Sexual identity   2. Sexual orientation 3. Social psychology
4. Sociology   5. Sociosexuality   6. Gender

DISCLAIMER
This book is a social science analysis and is no substitute for professional
medical, spiritual or psychological care. Medical, spiritual, psychological and all
professional help and counseling should be obtained from an appropriate
specialist in the field.

Karen Sinclair
P.O. Box 206
South Orange, NJ 07079
United States of America
www.karenswall.com

Cover designed by Ebook Launch

TABLE OF CONTENTS

Dedication vii

Acknowledgments ix

Preface xi

Introduction xvii

Chapter 1: Primary Perspectives 3
    Rose Bush Perspective 3
    The Orientation Bouquet 13
    Perspectives of Biology 17
    The Shape of Identity 19
    The Dominant Reality 24
    Culture of "Straights" 26
    Recognition 28

Chapter 2: Sociosexual Identity 33
    Social Environment and Identity 33
    Elements of Cultivated Sexual Identity 42
    Sexual hierarchy 43
    Nurturing and Controlling Sociosexual Identity 51
    Gender Based Behavior as Sociosexual Phenomena 56
    Institutionalized Sociosexual Codes 63
    Sociosexual Attraction 66

Chapter 3: Anatomy and Identity 71
    The Voice of Sexual Identity 71
    Cultivated Identity in Hair 72
    Muscle-- Sociosexual Cause or Effect? 74
    Revelation's "Bingo" and Biology 75
    Genes, hormones and DNA 77

Chapter 4: The Social Sentence of the Sexes 81
    Socioeconomic Perspectives 81
    The Sentence of Human Survival 84
    Education, Learning and the Sociosexual Sentence 92
    The Pool of Religious Perspectives and Beliefs 98

Chapter 5: The Sentence as Intellectual Activity 109
    Intellectual freedom vs. Biology 109
    Internet Dating—Revealing the Sexual Intellect 110
    Rejecting the Sentence 113
    Enjoying the Sentence 115

Chapter 6: Law, Policy and Rights 117
    American Equal Rights 117
    "Don't Ask Don't Tell" Military Policy 118
    Domestic Partnerships and Civil Unions 119
    Social Acceptance and Marriage 123
    Sexual Identity and Marriage 125

Chapter7: Social Convention and Practices **129**
  Conformity and non-conformity 129
  The Ice Cream Principle... 132
  Extelligence 134
  Behavioral Freedom- The New Morality 140
  Therapy 143
  Surgery 147
  Perspectives of Orientation... 151
  Gender, Identity and Orientation (gio) Indexes 156
Chapter 8: Beyond Sexual Horizons **167**
  Revisiting Human perception 167
  Distinguishing Learning from Biology... 168
  Habit and Lifestyle.. 170
  Man and his environment 176
  Conquest of the mind.. 178
Chapter 9: The Turf of Sexual Activity **183**
  Desire 183
  Love 185
  Availability 187
  Conscious Choice.. 188
  Force and persuasion 188
  Habit 189
  Physical Attraction.. 191
  Stimulation-- sensual.. 192
  Stimulation--physical.. 194
  Stimulation-- Drugs 196
Chapter 10: How it all comes together... **199**
Summary **203**
Conclusions... **207**
Appendix 1: Gender, Identity and Orientation Index Tables **216**
Appendix 2: List of Illustrations **217**
Appendix 3: Sexual Mosaic **219**
Index **220**
Bibliography **222**

DEDICATION

This book is lovingly dedicated to my mother, May Blackman, who stayed by my side every day throughout the many years it took to write it, then slipped into eternal grace just before I wrote the final chapter. To both my parents, May and Ovid Blackman, thank you for the values, the strength and the faith you nurtured in my life.

ABOUT WHOEVER

ACKNOWLEDGMENTS

I feel indebted to everyone whose documentation of aspects of the human condition has provided fodder for the analyses formulated in this book. Whether it was the report carried in a Time Magazine that the Archbishop of Canterbury, head of the global Anglican Communion, was seeking some kernel of consensus in liberal and conservative perspectives about homosexuality, or the more colorful newspaper reports of a "bathroom arrest" of an Idaho congressman or of a Michigan congresswoman censored for using the word "vagina", I was drawn to the need to understand human sexuality and various contemporary dimensions of sexual identity and orientation. Empirical news reports carried on PBS Television, CBS and NBC news, including interviews conducted by veteran reporters and interviewers, such as Barbara Walters and Oprah Winfrey, rang bells for the analyst in me about an issue to be clarified and understood. I am thankful for their experiential reports. Those simultaneous chimes signaled to me the dawn of a new age and I feel indebted to empirical media for paving the journey with information for this book.

Dr. Peter Jackson, Lecturer, Columbia University, School of Continuing Education and formerly Senior Editor at the United Nations, tirelessly edited my manuscript. His professional eye scrutinized the embryonic work and pinpointed defects that could have spoiled the quality of *About Whoever: The social imprint on identity and orientation.* For that, I am eternally grateful.

I would like to acknowledge the support of family and friends as well. Writing this book took several years and therefore intersected uncountable major and minor life events, including births, deaths, marriages, divorces, graduations, promotions and all kinds of celebrations and sorrows, many of them right under my own roof. Through this whole gestation period for the book, friends and family, like trusting parents before the days of amniocentesis, remained confident in its eventual birth. In particular, I would like to thank my sister, Paula Blackman, for her stoicism through the years of labor it took to deliver this book.

Perhaps my greatest acknowledgment is my gratitude to God for making it possible for me to write this book. I attribute the inspiration, innovative perspectives, novel theories and landmark conclusions to God. I stand up as the hands that did this, and accept any mistakes as all mine. As I struggled to understand the information I had gathered, I acknowledge not only seeking God's guidance, but also believing that I received it.

PREFACE

Firstly, *About Whoever: The social imprint on identity and orientation,* is not claiming that identity and orientation arise entirely from imprints of society, the people around us. It does claim that some elements deemed sexual are socially acquired or inspired. This book reflects contemporary observations of human sexuality and seeks to understand social and cultural elements of sexual behavior. I am writing with unknown influences of a Christian upbringing and perspective. Yet, my goal in this book is objective, analytical discussion. I am also writing in a period of upheaval concerning traditional values of human sexuality. In the distant past, we only recognized male and female and our vocabulary was largely built around the two, although other gender realities were acknowledged. Today, new legislation is being enacted, new social systems governing marriage and family are being proposed by legislators, scholars and citizens at large, and new value systems are emerging. As one listens to the debates about human sexuality, the many unanswered questions and grey areas and the emotion and fear that passionately separate decision makers, it seems that unemotional understanding may be the bridge to rational progress.

This analysis highlights the social imprint of human sexuality. It takes the perspective of social issues and phenomena and the environment of our social circumstances– culture, economics, politics, policy, technology and more. It adopts this perspective merely to facilitate closer examination and in no way proposes that other dimensions or perspectives do not exist.

In this writing, I have attempted to maintain an objective stand and hope that I have excluded opinions for which no proof can be cited. My aim is to present independent, objective information. Although the ideas, assessments and conclusions are my own, I have also shared perspectives available in literature on the subject and referenced these to advance discussions and to rationalize controversial points of view.

By avoiding unsubstantiated opinion, I am seeking to shape a rounded perspective. The resulting work may be of value to opposing points of view and have meaning to people of different even conflicting orientations, identities and beliefs. This objectivity promises a unifying work that brings both homosexual and heterosexual intelligence under a common umbrella. That is the goal. The unspoken assumption is that there is common ground.

The outlook in this book *About Whoever: The social imprint on identity and orientation* is that of an analyst trying to clarify and develop a positive understanding of the realities that could be helpful to the various deliberations. From debates in the Methodist church about whether gay ministers should be ordained; debates about whether a former Governor of New Jersey could be considered gay since he had long standing relationships with women, including two wives, before declaring himself gay; whether celibacy in the Catholic church predisposes men to relationships among themselves or whether it is the prospect of celibacy that attracts people, already pre-disposed to alternative lifestyles, to the catholic priesthood; whether it is discriminatory to permit marriage only between men and women; whether there is a third sex or other sexes; whether there are groups of people *choosing* a lifestyle that has historically been considered contrary to established social norms; whether there is in fact a dominant culture of "straights" monopolizing our lives from the beginning of documented history, and dominating laws and practices for no reason other than preservation of the "straights"; and to whether there is indeed a minority people who have been driven underground through history and historically been forced to thrive only in closets because of engendered social and legal biases. The debates are many, the interests diverse and goals of the debaters often incompatible. This book will attempt to replace bigotry, intolerance, partisan agenda, fear and confusion with understanding.

I see *About Whoever* as a *contribution* to truth; a *perspective* of truth, or ideally a magnifying glass, helping to provide clarity in the search for understanding. It is an attempt to sift through the doubts and gaps when these discussions are placed within the bigger picture. The analysis of the social imprint explores concepts of individuals and groups, society, culture, law, traditional and contemporary realities among other perspectives, and touches on biology in the search for an all-encompassing understanding, if there is one. Although biology defines the human body and may be considered an underlying factor in sexuality, the subject of this writing is more about the social imprint, cultural influences and nurturing environment and not about biological science. With this focus, biology is regarded as given. It is briefly discussed in terms of the way we interpret the given biology and use it in social and cultural contexts.

About Whoever: The social imprint on identity and orientation excludes discussion of evolutionary and ethological theories which also seek to interpret the evidence of human nature. This is not by any means an attempt to disrespect these theories. It is simply not within the scope of this book. The attempt here is to analyze, describe and document the place that sex, sexuality, sexual orientation and identity hold in contemporary society. The analysis is largely based on observations in North America. It is recognized that a wider research plateau may provide different perspectives.

I am also cautious of what William Wright in his book '*Born that Way*[i] referred to as "intellectual territoriality" that inspires the criticism of experts in a field.[1] Careful attempts have been made not to make judgmental conclusions and theories. There is therefore no judgment, no assessment of right or wrong, and no blanket prescription. It is my belief that we mortals merely have perspectives, we are not owners of truth.

The writer is aware of various theories and factions about human sexuality. However, this approach seeks to step away from pre-conceptions, biases and prejudices and the various camps of theories. It is a process of data and information gathering and analysis that seeks to describe perceived reality. Whether this process is flawed, you be the judge. If

---

[1] Wright, William, *Born that Way*, Alfred A. Knopf, Inc. New York, 1998, p. 176

this attempt is successful, hopefully it will add to the body of knowledge about sexuality and be of value to society.

Future scholarly research may build on some of the perspectives and separate particular ideas and theories to pursue in greater detail. Others may want to debate, dispute or challenge some of the ideas. That is progress. In the final analysis, whenever, or if that is ever achieved, *About Whoever: The social imprint on identity and orientation* would have made its contribution.

INTRODUCTION

Silent inspiration behind social communication and behavior is, more often than may be acknowledged, sex or a sexual reference. Sexual references pervade language, and underlie linguistics and social practices. At the same time, through censorship and social roles we are taught that sex is secret, and that explicit sexuality is impolite, vulgar and pornographic. Yet, inbred behaviors implicitly pay homage to our sexuality. In our social pursuits, we dress to highlight sexual differences and nurture distinct culturally appropriate behaviors for different sexes. Advertising, even for food and politics, uses veiled (and sometimes obvious) sex-based tactics. It is understood that sex gets attention, while occurrences and behavior that are prudish must exclude sex.

Indeed, sexuality has such a hold on society that although it underlies daily pursuits in many ways, many aspects of sex are considered unsuitable for discussion in polite conversation and in public media directed at general audiences today. Sexual content is made an issue in that programs and advertising are rated according to (among other things) the suitability of sexual content for general audiences. The United States Federal Communications Commission, (FCC) specifically prohibits the broadcast of obscene material *at any time* and allows indecent programming only during certain hours. In their guide to obscenity, indecency and profanity[2], the definitions of obscene and indecent include material that depicts or describes particular sexual conduct or sexual organs, among other things, and also relies on a measure of "contemporary community standards". Of significance in these FCC rules is the quest to avoid broadcast at times when there is a risk that children may be in the audience. Also of note is that these rules define obscenity to include sexual conduct. Under the threat of Federal Law, broadcasters risk losing their licenses to broadcast. Accidents, such as wardrobe malfunctions, may lead to severe fines for broadcasters. Guided by law, operators go to extremes, such as time delay broadcasting, to ensure that grass-roots terms for sexual intercourse (considered obscene) are not broadcast. These rules effect the silence. Such rules of silence govern the development and awareness of sexual identity and sexual orientation.

In contrast, education systems include rudiments of mathematics, grammar, the alphabet and numbers, which, at an early age equip children to function as literate beings. We expose children to intricacies of music and science, sophisticated technology and industry in games toys and formal classroom experience. Yet, the rudiments of human sexuality remain completely shrouded in this silence. So shrouded is sexuality that even adult perspectives have been conditioned to equate any partial nudity with sex, when seen

---

[2] http://www.fcc.gov/guides/obscenity-indecency-and-profanity, June 27, 2011

in the media. In this regard, the notion that "sex sells" is a popular guide to TV programming. The notion equates foreplay and partial nudity with sex in general programming without fully acknowledging that explicit sex is never broadcast in general programs because of the FCC rules of obscenity and vulgarity. Explicit sex causes programs to be labeled XXX rated and regulated to pornographic adult stations. This is also the case for websites and online channels. Sexting, the transmission of nude photographs by cell phone messaging, is considered obscene. As part of the contemporary community standard in the United States, nudity is considered an obscenity. The human body must be covered from the eyes of the young. This "contemporary community standard" is not specifically defined by the FCC. It appears to depend on public outcry and subjective monitoring by the FCC. It is therefore fluid and perpetual. In this way, we master the silence, censoring our own communication and "protecting" our children from every morsel of information about sex for as long as we could. The attitude appears to be that factors influencing the formation of sexual identity and sexual orientation need not be understood, need not be the subjects of formal education, and must be eliminated from main-stream social communication in American society. No one ever asks "why?" It is generally accepted that it is right and good to "protect" children from this information. It is a contemporary community standard in America. This comment is neither to challenge nor support the standard. It is merely to recognize and acknowledge what is a tacit agreement in the culture. Significantly, in 2012, a Michigan congresswoman was censored for using the word "vagina" in congress[3]. The mere use of this word in congress was such a newsworthy event that it was carried in international newspapers, such as in the United Kingdom.[4] In ways such as these, our formal systems nurture highly educated minds who understand how to clone sheep, successfully master brain surgery, and understand the rudiments of the physical body, while there is no understanding of the sexual being.

One result of our complicity in silence is that available information on sex is often monopolized by illegal sources and unsavory ventures. Through zoning and regulation sex is ostracized to the underground. Since our social practices encourage screening of publications and rating literature and art based on sexual content, subtle and overt sexual rules are established, and all are touched directly or indirectly by society. Silence begets ignorance. In recent American history, that ignorance has threatened presidencies and dethroned at least one governor and a top military officer. The first thing that we as a society can do to dispel the ignorance is to break that silence. Understanding and education may not only bring clarity to individuals threatened by ignorance and confusion, but also bridge the gulf separating liberal and conservative perspectives about human sexuality.

This book accepts the popular rainbow principle that there is a diverse array of sexual identities and orientations and seeks to understand the role society plays in this. *About Whoever* perceives that all spectra of the rainbow: straight,

---

[3] "Michigan Rep. Censored For Use Of 'V-Word'", http://detroit.cbslocal.com/, June 14, 2012
[4] "Eve Ensler and Lisa Brown to read Vagina Monologues in Michigan", http://www.guardian.co.uk/uk, June 16, 2012

gay, trans and whoever, are touched by society. To begin our discussion, let us introduce some of the terms we will be using most frequently in this book.

ABOUT WHOEVER

CHAPTER 1: PRIMARY PERSPECTIVES

Rose Bush Perspective

The word "gender" has significantly evolved from its pre-1990's Webster's dictionary definition as 'the classification by which words are grouped as feminine, masculine or neuter'[5].   Today's usage encompasses the traditionally acknowledged genders as well as contemporary gender states made possible both by advances in medical science and surgery and modern acceptance of all nature's gifts without exclusion or judgment.   We live in a time when previously unidentified/ unrecognized gender realities and definitions are being recognized.   Having in the past recognized masculine and feminine and built our vocabulary largely around the two, other genders such as 'hermaphrodite' for example, though acknowledged, were not accorded a similar place in the culture.   That is to say, it was considered an anomaly, a flaw or deformity in gender, which was considered to be either masculine or feminine only.   Within

---

[5] *Webster's New Dictionary and Thesaurus*, Windsor Court, NY, 1989

that framework, individual gender (a noun) is stated as either man or woman. Linguistically, the word 'hermaphrodite' was never complementary or pleasant. It was a state of being to be whispered, ostracized or pitied. Today, other terms such as *intersex* and *transex,* acknowledge gender beyond man and woman and receive acknowledgement and growing acceptance in popular media.

Though traditionally based on genitals, gender includes fundamental social cultural characteristics. To understand this statement, let us examine the rose bush analogy. Before it begins to flower, the rose bush is recognized by its thorns, leaves and the stem that we see. It helps you to categorize it and distinguish it from other kinds of plants. So too is gender. It gives us the terms to recognize individuals and distinguish them from other individuals. The Rose Bush Perspective of Gender recognizes man, woman and contemporary states including intersex (hermaphrodite-persons born with both male and female sex organs), and transex (acknowledging surgical change to the original biology).

Observed sex difference is articulated as gender and gives us adjectives 'male' and 'female'. In that sense, gender may be regarded a cultural acknowledgment of different sexes. It is cultural in that we *select* particular biological organs as representative of the core of gender and ignore others. We *assume* that those organs are the marks of distinction between the sexes. In other words, the understanding_is that those organs, not chromosomes, not DNA, not some other factor, but *those organs,* are conclusive indicators of gender. That traditional perspective of gender has lost universal acceptance. There are those who reject the primary presumption about male/ female biological gender. Today, gender descriptions are often used interchangeably with identity and orientation descriptions. However, whatever the basis of gender descriptions, gender is an attempt to categorize what you are, based on qualifying criteria. Today, gender categories and criteria are both changing.

Contemporary definition of gender is primarily based on sexual organs in virtually the same process that the rose bush is recognized by its thorns, leaves and stems. Even before it flowers, one knows that it is a rose bush and not, for example, a sunflower. In our culture, gender is similarly recognized based on the acknowledgment of particular traits. (Traits will be discussed in greater detail in the section Elements of Cultivated Sexual Identity.) Gender defines what distinct people categories exist. Beyond acknowledging the contemporary definitions, it is important from a social and cultural perspective to acknowledge the acceptance the categories male, female, intersex and transex enjoy. These terms follow historical perspectives about criteria. In popular usage today, the term 'gay' transcends acknowledgment of external sexual organs. It includes behavioral dimensions. Those who use the term to describe gender assert legitimacy beyond genitals, thereby implying that it takes more than genitals to be male or female. Today, studies of gender are extensive and include behavioral characteristics and interdisciplinary factors. Gender is of interest in this book in so far as it has an impact on human sexuality. Use of the term 'gay' in relation to gender includes acknowledgement of an individual's personal gender preference or gender behavior. This means that, while "male", "female", "intersex" and "transex" may be objectively understood empirically, 'gay' when used as a gender category, requires subjective information. It is up to the gay individual to come out. Individuals with the same physical and social characteristics and behaviors may define themselves differently and unless an individual "comes out", an observer cannot absolutely conclude that the person is gay.

Although other terms are often used, these terms are respectful references to particular contemporary genders. It is true that linguistic respect does not imply social acceptance. Different individuals, interest groups and segments of the community still despise, bully, denigrate and discriminate against some genders. However, given the burden old terms like "hermaphrodite" shouldered, the new terms must be acknowledged for their role in the path of social and cultural change.

These gender definitions are part of the social and cultural process in that they provide a handle for similar people to recognize each other. Cultural change may also be reflected in the acceptance of babies born with both genitals, who were historically the object of early 'corrective' surgery based on parental preference. No longer under pressure to make a baby conform to a pre-conceived dichotomous gender culture, parents and gynecologists confronted with an intersex baby may perhaps be less inclined to define the child as a freak. Acceptance of the term may therefore be a balm to medical 'intervention' and an important sociocultural mechanism.

While gender attempts to define *what* a person is based on criteria, in contrast, identity attempts to express *who* a person is. It relies on the individual's personal assessment (regardless of external biological features). Individual feelings, emotions and personal factors, including personal positions on gender may be reflected in identity and in 'coming out' about identity.

As the rose bush holds its flowering secrets until it begins to bud, so too are secrets of individual sexuality often undisclosed until maturity. Despite gender definitions that occur from birth, sexuality, the presence of a sexual dimension in an individual, typically becomes evident at puberty for all genders. Emerging sexuality may therefore be likened to the budding of a rose. As the rose buds, so too does human sexual identity begin to clarify. Although children may display varied sexual curiosities and behaviors prior to puberty, at that stage they are considered developmental and not necessarily conclusive about sexual identity. Sexual identity clarifies birth gender and has historically been expected to be consistent at puberty with birth gender: boys becoming men and girls becoming women at puberty. However, today we may distinguish that identity from gender. The term 'gender identity', coined by psychologist Robert Stoller[ii] in the 1960s, in his book *Sex and Gender: On the Development of Masculinity and Femininity*, helps us to acknowledge the cultural acceptance of identity consistent with birth gender as defined, as well as identity based on gender as perceived through other social and cultural standards, norms and emerging preferences and through self identity.

7

When the color of the budding rose begins to emerge, just as individual gender blossoms into identity, the pigment red or white, pink or yellow appears, parallel to biological, social and emotional changes of adulthood. At the moment, the linguistic culture that influences the description of emerging identity is diverse. Terms referring to similar definitions of individual identity including heterosexual or straight, homosexual or, gay, lesbian, Same Gender Loving, SGL, and terms such as androsexual, gynosexual, transsexual and so forth are statements of individual nature beyond gender. Those terms are names, not criteria. They group similar identities but do not help us to understand them. Historically, identity was based on gender. Today people often assert sexual identity based on evidence of sexual interest in others, which is an aspect of sexual orientation. Terms like SGL (Same Gender Loving), change the perception of gender and identity from reflections of biology, to reflections of emotion. In that sense, the terms move love to the forefront of identity and gender discussions which had previously been focused on sex. Even the traditional terms 'heterosexual' and 'straight, are evaluative (of orientation) more than they are descriptive of identity. When identity descriptions include reference to relationships with others, people are identified based on their orientation. As flowering color clarifies the imperceptive secret of the generic rose bush, so too does identity clarify gender. Rose bush color, is a helpful perspective in distinguishing individual identity from gender, but the similarities between the two end here. Whereas the rose bush color is whatever you see, individuals have a say in their identity regardless of apparent gender. Gender-based sexual identity includes male/ female/

transgender/ transsexual/ intersexual which acknowledge the original gender definition. These incorporate assumptions about identity as boys become men and girls become women.

When the color of the budding rose begins to emerge, just as individual gender blossoms into identity, the pigment red or white, pink or yellow appears, parallel to biological, social and emotional changes of adulthood.

Figure 1: Rose Bush Perspectives

In contrast, sociosexual identity is inclusive of identity consistent with or different from gender. Intersex gender may bud into either male or female identity or remain intersexed in identity, never relinquishing either. Identity of transgender individuals is similar to intersexuals who hold on to both male and female gender identities, differing only in that the original gender is not intersex. Transexuals blossom with identities opposite to birth gender.

In addition to choosing terminology, individuals today choose how and if they would like to be defined by their sexuality. For example some transsexuals further clarify their status by identifying as transsexual male or transsexual female; and intersexuals (having both male and female sexual organs/ dispositions) sometimes choose to identify as intersexual male or intersexual female as appropriate for them.

In recent times, clarifications of sexual identity may have become increasingly important because so much social life occurs not in person, but in a virtual environment. With the advent of social networking, opportunities abound for virtual connections that are text based rather than flesh based. In this regard, social networks provide (among a myriad of other things) *pseudo*social opportunities for individuals to make connections in order to pursue sexual relationships. To be successful in this quest, the internet generation must define their sexual interest as precisely as possible, so that they may connect with those whose interests are compatible or complementary. On the Internet, in chat rooms and Internet dating sites, people search and find each other based on words, browse photographs, text and videos, and initiate and build relationships through virtual (non-physical) channels. Whether related to the technology or not, the terminology to express and define sexual identity has become more specific over the years. This is explored further in later discussions on orientation and the formulation of 'gio indexes' in the section titled Gender, Identity and Orientation (gio) Indexes.

Terms used to define sexual identity are only one dimension. Sexual identities include a wide spectrum of culturally defined and definable sexual states combining a complex kaleidoscope of characteristics and individual preferences. In other words, despite whatever gender may be observed and whether that identity is or is not consistent with that gender, individuals in our culture have a say and may choose to express sexual identities in a variety of ways. The individual, not any process, is the final and only determinant of that identity. For example, the cultural practice of "coming out" is an occasion when an individual makes known his sexual identity. Beyond that, it is a cultural offense for anyone to suggest or presume another person's sexual identity. Today, there is an unofficial 'right' to self identity. In practice, no proof is required and no standard needs to be met. Once declared in a "coming out" event, one's sexual identity is asserted.

It is a cultural truth that heterosexual individuals do not "come out", neither do they generally identify themselves based on sexuality. This is not surprising. Because this is a time of cultural change with regard to our historically heterosexual culture, the decision to publicly declare sexual identity is almost exclusively not heterosexual. In my view, this may be an important aspect of identity and of community development based on identity. Community development advocates may need to be aware that the voices heard in the community may not necessarily be representative of the community, since some voices may be more inclined to speak out. Silence on one issue or another may therefore not necessarily mean acquiescence. People on all sides, whether heterosexual or not, may be more expressive about the culture that is <u>not</u> the historical standard. This may not mean that the historic standard is understood in the community, nor that the particular community has any commitment to or against the historic standard. Instead, it may merely be that those who are silent have no perception of a culture *other than* the traditional heterosexual culture and do not feel the same urge to speak.

Significantly, size of membership population has been a factor in the development and survival of historical communities. Today, the emerging challenger against the historically heterosexual culture often identifies as lesbian/ gay/ bisexual/ transsexual or LGBT. This binds together into a single community, sexual communities *outside of* the heterosexual tradition. The shape of contemporary sexual identity may be influenced by this factor in that it presupposes some form of inclusiveness. It presupposes "all". Within definitions of the path to acceptance, such an assumption could shape the new culture since it creates two camps, straight and LGBT and it is expressed *as if* all were included.

That is not to suggest that declaration is acceptance. Partisan interests, including political and religious influences, shape acceptance. But acceptance is another dimension of the social imprint that will be discussed separately, in the section "Elements of Cultivated Sexual Identity".

The Orientation Bouquet

So far, we have discussed gender in terms of criteria analogous to the rose, and identity as a function of qualities we declare about who we are. Continuing the rose bush analogy, all identities taken together would represent a sexual bouquet. Orientation surrounds relationships among individuals in the sexual bouquet.

Discussing sexual orientation is equivalent to taking all the full bloomed roses and examining their relationships with each other. The term *orientation* encompasses individual relationships with others, tendencies of behavior toward each other and observance of a historical standard. In terms of the rose analogy, not only is it true that all pink roses do not display the same shade of pink, but there are many varieties of rose, given names such as "Black Magic" to distinguish them. So too, there is a rainbow array of different 'varieties' of sexual orientation. Categories, such as straight/ heterosexual/ gay/ lesbian/ homosexual/ bisexual/ same gender loving, are expressive of the cultural array of contemporary sexual orientation. Clearly, orientation and identity are related. While identity is an individual matter, orientation as the word implies, includes tendencies and inclinations. Its relationship with identity is in regard to a perception of an individual's relationships with others. For example, a person may be male (gender), but bisexual (orientation), But in cultural practice, orientation can be different from identity and distinct from gender: A person may be male (gender), but may assert identity as female, and be homosexual in orientation. This cultural incidence may appear incomprehensible to some, but clarifies that his role in a relationship is *oriented to* the role culturally seen as female. It will be explored further in the section Gender, Identity and Orientation (gio) Indexes.

The understanding of gender, identity and orientation is aided by evidence of transgender families presented on the Oprah Winfrey show of October 12, 2007. It brought to light the case that someone who identifies as a transgender female, but whose original gender was man, could nevertheless express sexual interest toward relationships with females. He changed gender but remained in relationship with the woman in his life. Had he not changed gender, his relationship with that same female would have been considered traditional. What occurred is that in his life as a male (gender), his identity was that of female. Having changed his gender to female, his identity and gender are the same. His ongoing relationship which was a traditional heterosexual relationship is now same sex. Similarly, one can understand that an intersexed person for example, may express an orientation toward or interest in male, female or intersexed individuals. It has also been observed that people defining themselves as male express interest in/ orientation toward intersexual or transsexual connections. These empirical and theoretical illustrations highlight the distinction between sexual identity and sexual orientation.

In our culture, individual orientation can remain a private matter and may not necessarily be a fixed constant. The evidence that people do declare that they had been in denial about their orientation appears to reflect this. Evidence that an individual may declare one identity and secretly pursue behaviors consistent with a different orientation is confirmation of orientation's elusiveness. While identity is an assertion, orientation need not be. Orientation is defined by tendencies and preferences in connection with others. Whether these tendencies and preferences are emotional, psychological, social or behavioral, or have some other influence, is not at issue here. The meaning is that the presence of some tendency or preference characterizes sexual orientation.

It is also a social reality that orientation may also not be reflected in behavior. The behavior described as being on the "down low" is also worth acknowledging in this discussion. In this practice, an individual asserts a particular sexual identity and *secretly* practices different behaviors. Examples of this behavior were publicly aired on the Oprah Winfrey television show in 2004, where an individual identified as J.L. King was profiled[6]. Individuals on the "down low" may identify themselves as heterosexual and maintain heterosexual lifestyles, including traditional families, but secretly pursue homosexual relationships. Such individuals are *actively* heterosexual in one context and *actively* homosexual in another (secret) context. The gender is male, the sexual orientation is essentially bisexual, but the behaviors and identities vary. The individual switches identities in the different contexts and pursues behaviors consistent with the *contextual* identity. This reality highlights the separation of orientation from identity. It

---

[6] Oprah Winfrey show, April 16th 2004

also shows how identity may be donned according to social contexts.

An interesting footnote is that, while this behavior is documented in the black community, it does not receive the same acknowledgement in other communities. This is not to suggest that *race* is an influence on sexual behavior, but that *community* is. The level of permissiveness afforded within the community may shape the variety of sexual behaviors that come to light. The desire of those who admit 'down low' behavior is to disguise their sexual pursuits and keep them below the social radar. A society which is permissive about a menu of sexual activities without requiring individuals to commit to any particular identity may see less secretive activity.

It is not merely that orientation is a secret; it is often a mystery that unfolds first for the individual and may or may not be consistent with identity. That is to say, since gender-identity is often pre-pubescent, and orientation confirmed through behaviors and awakenings in adulthood, the two may bloom at different stages of life. Acknowledging individual sexual orientation is acknowledgement of factors beyond gender and developments beyond the cradle. It facilitates recognition within the species and interactions among people.

In the following discussion the generic biology as well as the blooming process that produces the mature sexual person, will be discussed in general terms to enhance our understanding about our sexual traditions.

Perspectives of Biology

> *...our traditions color our perceptions, how we see*
> *each other and what helps us to define the*
> *biological male and female.*

There are two dimensions of biology that are pertinent to this discussion.   First, there is the perceived biology, including our organs, our muscles hair, genitals, torso and limbs etc., that is visible to the naked eye. Then there is the aspect of meaning, what these visible elements or organs that we recognize as sexual biology, denote to us. We will address these perspectives here.

The confusion with much of what we consider truth is that all it is, is a representation of reality as we know it, a perspective. We assert as a truth that all men are created equal. Then we presume meaning in our 'equal' biology. In other words, we take the obvious evidence and attach particular significance to it. For example, in the first half of the twentieth century, Gordon Childe, in his book *Man Makes Himself,*[iii] highlighted the difference between social heritage and biological inheritance[7]. He points to our activities and behaviors that are not inherited but learned and also showed how we are in control of their adoption. He wrote:

> *Changes in culture and tradition can be initiated,*
> *controlled, or delayed by the conscious and deliberate*
> *choice of their human authors and executors. An*
> *invention is not an accidental mutation of the germ plasm,*

---

[7] Childe, Gordon, *Man Makes Himself,* The New American Library, New York, 1936, p.20

17

*but a new synthesis of the accumulated experience which
the inventor is heir by tradition only.*[8]

This may be taken to mean that changes in culture may not
necessarily be an unconscious progression, but may be
affected by conscious assessments guided by existing
traditions. We can extend this understanding to our sexual
biology to explain how our traditions color our perceptions,
how we see each other and what helps us to define male and
female. In that regard, we see the undeniable biology.
However, we attach significance to it based on our
traditions. Ultimately, we make either unconscious or
deliberate assessments or choices in relation to the traditions
we follow.

On the other hand our physical development is not
controlled by our consciousness. Regardless of our social
heritage and our attitudes, physical development is different
in boys and girls, including breast development and the
biological features mentioned in the earlier part of this
book. These are obvious features we have no trouble
acknowledging. Based on the traits our traditions cause us
to acknowledge, we look for and expect particular features
and set them up as the norm while we ignore others. We
also translate this biology into traditions of sex
identification.

Although the western world acknowledges gender
differences from birth, and encourages gender based activity
throughout development, it does not condone sexual activity
until after puberty. So these gender definitions, including

---

[8] Childe, Gordon, *op. cit.* p. 21

but not limited to our sexual organs, are not *actively* sexual. The practice in the western world is to delay sexual activity until the emergence of emotional maturity. In this sense, sexual activity is *value* based. To understand that this is not biology but a value, we may note that in some value systems it is not an age, but acquiring a particular status, such as marriage, that makes sexual activity acceptable. To support our value system, parents often screen children from conversations about sex and sexual development until they anticipate or observe impending sexual maturity or readiness. That is our tradition, our value system. We cover up the sexual parts of our bodies. We consider it harmful to expose children to sexual information. Movies with sexual content, books and magazines, discussions, and programs are restricted, veiled, hidden and flagged for parental guidance. Sex becomes the secret of all time, the magnet of all curiosity, anxiety, fear, doubt, confusion and insecurity. In other words, although we are labeled from birth, our social actions are encouraged to be asexual until puberty. Not so our social development. Socially, the label 'boy' or 'girl' is used to identify us, groom our identity and shape us for different roles in society.

The Shape of Identity

... How we see ourselves within or outside of the frame created by social processes

In this scenario identity then becomes a figment of our perception, shaped by the factors that society recognizes. In this vein, identity evolves not as an objective right of birth, or a stamp of our genes and heredity, but from how we see ourselves within or outside of the frame conjured and created by social processes. It is not an independent feature of our person, but a personal and subjective decision we each make about who we are. We are not born with an identity, but with an assembly of body parts and spiritual and mental capacities. Some of those are systematically highlighted, defined and identified through socialization.

A PBS news report in 2006 documented the case of the Ulas family in a remote Turkish village, whose five younger members walked on both hands and feet[9]. This is an extreme case, but it is presented here to demonstrate the relationship between identity and social nurturing. Their behavior, walking on all fours, is not the behavior expected of human beings. Today, it is accepted that one of the "natural" characteristics of the human, is walking upright. Yet, here is an entire family walking on all fours. It raises the question concerning how much of what we see as human, as natural, as normal development, is social and cultural. It raises our awareness that *even what we consider 'normal'* development, could instead be *cultural* development. The Ulas family was large, close in age, and socially isolated. It is surmised that because the children did not receive the usual nurturing provided in our culture, they did not ever learn to walk upright.

We do not fully understand the nature of the relationship between nurturing and individual development. It is not easy to see how or when it happens. Yet, it is our relationships and interactions with each other that keep us "human" and define for us what it means to be human. The

---

[9] PBS Television Broadcast, November 14, 2006

subtleties of nurturing make that almost indecipherable. If we can appreciate the consequences of lack of nurturing, (as demonstrated in the case of the Ulas family) perhaps we can see more clearly our contributions to it. We may also observe the effects of lack of nurturing in solitary confinement (the phenomenon observed when a prisoner is left without human companions in a confined cell) and hostage syndrome (the phenomena experienced when a hostage who has only captors as companions, begins to identify with those captors).

Illustrations of how identity can change are observed in both solitary confinement and hostage syndrome. People in solitary confinement lose or change their identity, may even develop behaviors seen as mental illnesses. Similarly, hostages begin to identify with their captors. After some period of association, a hostage, being deprived of the usual social associations, moves from a situation of fear to one of alignment with the captors. In both these situations, it is typically the *circumstance* that prompts people to change identity. Solitary confinement and captivity remove freedom from the normal social dynamic and affect the state of the individual. We also know that in cases such as schizophrenia, people find comfort in aligning with identities that relieve them of some trauma.

The point of this discussion is to examine circumstances where definitive identities can be scrutinized and identity changes occur. It is acknowledged that these are situational, not typical circumstances. However, they are referred to in the absence of real-time opportunity to isolate the usual process of identity development and change. Growth and development are slow processes that occur over years. These extraordinary circumstances are laboratory-like opportunities to help us unravel aspects of the process and to understand and recognize *the capacity* of the human intelligence to be influenced by environment. Understanding this capacity is a precursor to understanding some aspects of identity.

In particular, it helps us to appreciate that gender, identity and orientation are not immune to environmental influence in normal human development. This is not to say that either gender, identity, or orientation is environmentally determined. Not at all. This addresses a source of *potential influence* and affirms that during development, and *even in maturity,* as demonstrated by hostage syndrome, the influence of factors external to ourselves must not be discounted or underestimated. What we learn from the Ulas family, from hostage behavior and from prisoner behavior supports the perspective that the 'normal' human development that we assume to be based on some genetic factor, could instead be shaped by our society and culture. Even in basic human behavior, such as walking upright, *we do not know* where the role of genetics ends and where the influence of society begins. By extension, our shared values and shared nurturing are so integrated with the history of who we are that we perceive nurtured traits as parts of our biology. Even fundamental biological features of humans, such as walking upright, show social interdependence. The Ulas family experience opens the door to the thinking that walking is a social skill that we train our muscles and our brains to perform, much like the way that driving a vehicle can seem natural to the expert driver Notably, people have to re-learn to walk after a brain injury or after being physically laid up. Our gait, coordination, balance and related automatic and 'natural' movements are walking habits that become and are part of our nature. These examples raise questions about whether the sum total of what we consider human is a genetic/ biological *state,* or dynamic conditions of *being.*

The question about whether what is human is a *state* or acts of *being* may be applied to the understanding of gender identity and orientation. In the case of gender identity, we are assigned one from birth based on our society's values and perceptions, an *interpretation* of what is observed. Those values also shape how the identity is nurtured. Later, it is *being,* –behavior and tendency that enter discussions about orientation. This means that, although there is the instinctive attempt to align gender, identity and orientation, *the processes of arriving at each of these are not logically aligned.* There is misalignment or dissonance in that one is assigned using early observation, then nurtured, and the other reflects a conclusion arrived at later in life using a completely different perspective. The dissonance among the processes is consistent with the evidence that later in life, some individuals develop or perceive identities different from those originally assigned.

Has there ever been a challenge to the process of declaring sexual identity at birth? Since society has moved to be inclusive of a wider spectrum of sexual identity and orientation, it becomes important to distinguish infant gender declaration from the mature sexual declaration. The dissonance seems to be in the social *expectation* associated with the interpretation of the evidence at birth. The sex or gender may be biologically determined, but sexuality is cultural expression. This is explored further in later discussions of extelligence in Chapter 7: Social Convention and Practices.

The Dominant Reality

"...the world presents us not with unequivocal facts but with factors that we interpret and debate"

Ian Stewart & Jack Cohen

In the western world, we define as real those things that we can perceive with our acknowledged senses—sight, hearing, touch. If we can see it, hear it or touch it, we consider it real. So in our attempts at understanding phenomena, we try to reduce them to these realities. For example, we collectively acknowledge the biology we see. Scientists dissect and analyze and look for relationships, effects, and causes that can be demonstrated within that framework. We include those findings in our "real world". We then derive "facts" from this real world. If it can't be demonstrated, it is considered illogical, unscientific. As Ian Stewart and Jack Cohen explain in their book *"Figments of Reality"*, the world presents us not with unequivocal facts but with factors that we interpret and debate.[10] Albert Einstein is credited with having expressed similar ideas: "The truth of a theory is in

---

[10] Stewart, Ian, and Cohen, Jack, *Figments of Reality*, Cambridge University Press, Cambridge, 1997, p. 33

your mind, not in your eyes."[11] So the question becomes, who controls this reality, our thinking and interpretation?

In almost any society and in almost any time in history some dominant stratum of humanity could be found (usually including those who make the laws) that strives and exists at the expense of other groups of people. These are usually strata that intentionally or unintentionally create laws and propagate values that promote themselves and preserve their status. They shape the society, our thoughts, values and attitudes. History provides evidence of various degrees of religious, economic, social or political dominance, as well as discrimination against slaves, women, black people, in fact against people of some color, race, creed, sexuality, language, accent, size etc. or who differ in some way from the dominant class or segment of the society. Extreme documented examples include an early Egyptian king who sought to exterminate all male babies of Israeli descent in order to exert the dominance of Egyptians[12]. History also documents three hundred years of enslavement of people of African descent in a worldwide system that subjugated people based on color. Even contemporary society is rife with documented systems of discrimination such as that against the Dalits of India and the indigenous people of the Congo. The point is: the existence of systems of dominance controlled by a class of people is a known social reality. One may conclude that dominance occurs not because of the innate characteristics of that difference, but the recognition of some distinct factor and the establishment of a system of

---

[11] Einstein, A., qtd. In, Eves, H. *Mathematical Circles Squared,* Prindle Weber & Schmidt, Boston, 1972, taken from
http://math.furman.edu/~mwoodard/ascquote.html
[12] *King James Bible,* Exodus, Chapter 1-2

exploitation based on social rules and cultural practices that diminish the validity of a group of people. These practices become norms that over time are labeled 'natural' within particular social contexts.

The dominant reality exerts such comprehensive influence that unconscious behavior that may seem natural is often learned behavior. The way people think further influences differences that are reinforced; how we define and see ourselves and each other, and also whether we like ourselves and each other. This is encompassed in our social and cultural heritage. It is our reality. Our "facts" and "truths" are perceptions and horizons defined by dominant culture, whether we are aware of it or not. It is the context not only of our value systems and our sense of right and wrong, but more importantly our perception of ourselves and the world around us.

Culture of "Straights"

> ...The culture defines and classifies people and prescribes roles and behaviors based on male or female expectations of gender

The recognition of difference is a means of advancement for dominant strata and helps to enforce the influence that one group can exert over another in advancing some cause. In other words, if there had been no recognition of different sexes, there would be no way to prescribe male and female social roles, career choices, or salary differences. Instead, leaders in the western world are predominantly male, and the white race continues to exert dominance over the populations it formerly enslaved. For example, even with declared and constitutional pledges of equality, American society is conscious of and acts on dominant racial and other differences: Power through domination is also part of how we define and recognize our sexuality. We regard domination as natural– not what is the domination, but how we recognize it, how we define it. When it comes to our sexuality, ours is in essence a dominant culture of "straights"– a culture that defines and classifies people and prescribes roles and behaviors based on male/ female gender definitions. In other words, it is a culture dominated by heterosexuals. Stemming from this, our reality presumes gender, seeks gender and most compellingly, demands gender.

The historical presumption is that there is gender in each person that is consistent across the human race and that each person is either male or female. That is a fundamental presumption that pervades our culture. It is what we consider 'natural'. Even the new gender identities that have emerged since Webster last defined gender as male and female, support the quest for gender. Individual life outside of gender is inconceivable.

Within the presumption of gender is the compulsion for sexual identity. Gender is not only presumed, it must be assumed. In our culture, to fit in, there must be some sexual identity.

Recognition

> *...recognition and acknowledgement could*
> *influence how children are affirmed (or not) and*
> *how they proceed*

If we concur with the ideas about our perception of the world as expressed by Ian Stewart and Jack Cohen in "Figments of Reality,[13] we can appreciate how as a society we tacitly agree to accept social gender based roles. It is simply that we share current perceptions. As a culture, we recognize gender and use that recognition to characterize and define roles and behavior.

Cultural systems are defined not only by behaviors and roles, but also by the methods of controlling and ensuring those behaviors. In the case of gender based roles, these methods include ridicule of young children and this can escalate into violence as children age. These systems and methods of control are in place to assure that the expected behaviors are preserved as the norm. For example, some female children get type cast as "tom boys" and boys as "girlie men" to use popular pejorative clichés, because of activities they enjoy and behaviors inconsistent with cultural expectations prescribed for their gender. Pejorative terminology is one form of control that serves to preserve the cultural expectations. In addition to those 'big stick' methods, positive reinforcement techniques in the form of compliments and rewards encourage the behaviors. The question is: what makes a predilection for toy cars and climbing trees masculine? What makes playing dolls house

---

[13] Stewart & Cohen, *op. cit.* p.33

feminine? Further, is either sexual? Whatever it is, mere recognition and acknowledgement could influence how children are affirmed (or not) and how they proceed. Reward and punishment is one way in which the sexual culture is maintained.

Language is one means by which sexual culture is communicated. In the examples above, the rewards and punishments are bestowed through language.

It is through language for example that we establish the role of sex in our culture. Words in everyday social use highlight the silent influence of the sexual context. One such word 'vulgar', which may be applied to loud behavior, literally originates as an adjective meaning 'of the common people' attributed to the Latin word for 'people'. Over time, the silent master, sex, gained dominance in the meaning. It is in contemporary use, not merely a social assessment of people. Instead, today the very definition of what is socially acceptable versus what is "vulgar" pertains to sex. The Encarta Dictionary of North American English highlights a particular link with sex or bodily functions, in the meaning of the word. Subtly in our language we categorize sex as common, crude and vulgar. Similarly, "indecent exposure" is language pertaining to sex-based behavior. Pornography, the container of sexually explicit material, is unfavorably regarded. So, we are taught, sex is secret and explicit sexuality is impolite, vulgar or pornographic. Yet, our behavior implicitly pays homage to our sexuality.

On the subject of recognition, language has a subconscious dimension. It is a subliminal vehicle of gender recognition and subconsciously conveys through the ages this gender preoccupation or compulsion in our culture. For example,

29

in some cultures such as French, Spanish, Italian, to name just a few, gender is assigned through language, even to inanimate objects. We see this echoed in both the French and Spanish assigning the feminine "La" to the inanimate object 'table'. This is just one instance of human *gender compulsion*—the urge to assign gender– that is an important element in shaping the individual identity. In our identity, it is vital to pronounce gender. In this sense language is an element of sociosexual diplomacy. One must use appropriate pronouns communicating gender even in ordinary conversations.

Although this is one role of language in the maintenance of our sexual culture, language is only the beginning of the process of positively (or negatively) reinforcing the culture.

Various control behaviors reinforce systems of recognition and the associated roles. These behaviors and systems nurture receptive minds to identify with acceptable behaviors or to reject unacceptable behaviors and in so doing shape and define individuals. That is what makes culture- people acting in agreement, in sync, sharing and repeating behaviors that become custom. Superimposed on what we recognize is therefore a cultural perspective. This includes systematically nurtured attitudes and patterns of how people identify themselves and how others recognize and identify them. Identity and its recognition are not merely issues of biology. It is a social issue, constructed of the built-in rules that have for millennia been systematically maintained.

Recognition includes those dimensions that are selected, as well as the rules that help to maintain that selection. In the discussion of identity, it includes not only practices that ensure that there always is some form of gender identity, but also practices that maintain the recognition of gender throughout life along with particular external signs enabling people to recognize and identify each other socially.

CHAPTER 2: SOCIOSEXUAL IDENTITY

Recognition and definition of individual sexual identity using socially acquired characteristics is an accepted tradition.

Social Environment and Identity

We learn that individual personalities are molded by social processes. As Edward Wilson explains it in his book *On Human Nature*[iv]:

> *Each person is molded by an interaction of his environment, especially his cultural environment, with the genes that affect social behavior.*[14]

This perception merges environment, genes and behavior to shape an individual person. Included in this shaping are individual gender and identity. When we defined gender and distinguished it from identity in the first chapter, no cause, origin or responsibility for fashioning either was identified. Social environment is just one complex,

---

[14] Wilson, Edward O., *On Human Nature*, Harvard University Press, Cambridge, 1978, p.18

multifarious component. While it does not *determine* sexual identity, social environment influences and encourages sexual identity and often orientation. Evidence of this is reflected in several socio-cultural phenomena, including our communication styles, names, birth and other traditions, and our language, many of which assign gender, and shape our lifestyles. These will be addressed in Chapter 7: Social Convention and Practices and Chapter 8: Beyond Sexual Horizons.

The importance of gender identity is evident in many of our social practices, often beginning even before birth. In some modern cultures for example, one accepted practice is that parents seek to ascertain the gender of their babies *before* birth, often for the sole purpose of making the appropriate social preparations– purchasing the right colors, and preparing new nurseries in the appropriate color schemes. These social practices are partly self-sustaining. Handing down these traditions establishes them as important to us. To the extent that those colors and this preparation are not birth rights, but a socially established norm, which recognizes socially appropriate gender differences, *sexual* identity is given *social* value.

It has already been established in Chapter 1 that we are born with a recognizable *biology,* but like the hidden rose bush color, not born with a *known* or a fully blown, overt sexuality. That sexuality, the phenomena described by many names such as heterosexual, homosexual, gay, lesbian, same gender loving, SGL, androsexual, gynosexual, transsexual, is not visible at birth. Instead, we are born with an assembly of body parts, spiritual and mental capacities, yet to be revealed. Sexuality is also yet to be revealed. The label of sexual identity that our culture is inclined to apply is also yet to be attached. At birth we just *are*, without labels or tags. Birth records do not say '6-pound baby boy, gay'. It is our social processes that not only *interpret* some aspect of that 'assembly', but also assign meaning and value– that is, an identity– to it. For example, if a child is born with both sexual organs, doctors have historically tried to "fix" that child so that the child can fit in socially. It is interpreted as a medical problem. Dr. Alice Dreger who looked at a full spectrum of intersex related concerns listed the following concerns in response to the question of whether intersexed genitals are a medical problem:

> *Yes. Untreated intersex is highly likely to result in depression, suicide, and possibly "homosexual" orientation. Intersexed genitals must be "normalized" to whatever extent possible if these problems are to be avoided.[15]*

Further, in assessing the concealment centered model of the correct medical response in this comparison, Dr. Dreger cited elimination of psychological distress as the reason for the recommended "normalization":

> *The correct treatment for intersex is to "normalize" the abnormal genitals using surgical, hormonal, and other technologies. Doing so will eliminate the potential for parents' psychological distress.[v]*

In assessing patient centered concerns Dr. Dreger points out that intersexed genitals are not diseased. She referred to urinary tract infections and metabolic disorders as possible problems of a true medical nature. This outlook is consistent with the understanding of the role of society in

---

[15] Dreger, Alice, PhD, "Shifting the Paradigm of Intersex Treatment", Intersex Society of North America, September 25, 2007

shaping our identities. Granted that surgery may avert serious psychological and social problems later in life, I would venture that those psychological problems are not caused by the biological difference but by society's inability to nurture such a child. Particularly when the genitals are not diseased and pose no medical threat, I would also venture that both the psychological problems and the surgical approach in these situations are two different manifestations of a single social phenomenon—the presumption of heterosexuality previously discussed, and the related expectation that there are just two sexes. That same social process nurtures what it interprets. The process instills an expectation of two distinct sexes. It is geared to identify and interpret specific gender clues and has difficulty addressing those clues that do not follow expectations. Census data do not include records of births other than male and female. In addition, because doctors do not know in the undeveloped child, which is the "correct" sex (if there is one), and doctors know that they do not know, it is often not a medical decision. The parent may make the choice. Any choice based on personal social preferences further imposes social influences on the sexual tag that will characterize the development of the child. Another dimension worth noting here is that the expectation of two distinct sexes re-enforces itself in this process by eliminating the cases that do not conform to the expectation.

It is also interesting to note that Dr. Dreger's conclusions about the child's "abnormal genitals" cite the parent's expected psychological distress as justification for the surgery. One wonders if there is any other situation in which a doctor appears to advise surgery for someone in deference to the whim or state of mind of someone else. Even more significant is that this professional opinion was expressed in 2007, at none other than the "intersex society of America". Those factors hold important keys to the complexity of sociosexual culture. The practice of normalization trims human biology down to the expected culture. In keeping with this, census data need not acknowledge that these people were ever born. Having trimmed away the biology, the culture asserts the enforced reality that biological sex includes only male and female. The United States Census Bureau, for example, justifies maintaining statistics only for men and women based on a definition that refers to this normalized biology, asserting that "sex is based on the biological attributes of men and women"[16].

Sociosexual perspectives pervade our entire existence. First, society uses genitals to define and make conclusions about an active sexuality. From birth, the genitals, and only the genitals are equated with the sex. (Interestingly, we use the same approach with our pets and other animals and even wait (in the case of animals where the genitals are not initially visible) to pronounce gender after genitals develop.) Social processes similarly ignore some aspects of our being, however prominent they may be, making them insignificant components of that identity. Since other aspects of our being are considered secondary to genital identification, these social perspectives propagate the fantasy that sexuality is only a biological reality.

.

---

[16] United States Census Bureau, "Distinction between the concepts of gender and sex", http://www.census.gov/population/age/about/

Wilson described identity as the cultural environment interacting with genes. That is the essence of the sociosexual identity. It extends into many social rules such as those governing social norms based on sexual identity.

Among the most obvious are the rules that govern naming the sexes. This cultural norm assigns different first names for different sexes– another way we assign and communicate sexual identity. The effect of this convention is that our culture is charged with unspoken rules about names and gender such that even when one hears many names for the first time, one is usually able to guess the gender of the holder of the name. Of course, there are some exceptions, such as the use of gender neutral names, and cases where people do not follow the unspoken rules or habits of usage and give their sons traditional girls' names or their daughters traditional boys' names. It is more the norm to uphold than to violate the cultural practice of assigning first names consistent with the observed gender. These embedded gender clues in the first names given to children establish one label of our sociosexual identity—a social tradition that labels our sexual identity. The name often seals the birth gender declaration like a life sentence. A sentence served (with joy or despair) for the rest of one's life.

Neither the sociosexual sentence nor naming conventions are merely North American or English traditions. Other cultures and sub cultures around the world, western, eastern, European, and others have systems by which male and female names can be distinguished. For example Spanish names ending in –o or –a often indicate male and female identities respectively, such that Julia and Julio are instant gender statements, as are the East Indian names Vandana and Venkatharavan. It may very well be a universal practice across all cultures. Interestingly, when someone wants to change their sexual identity, changing the name is often one of the early steps toward a new identity—a valid social step that in our civilization asserts sexual identity. It is not a trivial matter. Names help individuals to fuse social and sexual identities. Evidence of this was found in a much publicized event in 2002, when an employee in a major New Jersey financial services firm changed gender[17]. In addition to assuming other trappings, the name Mark was changed to Maggie in transition to a new sexual identity. This was a social, psychological and sexual hurdle all at the same time.

Interpreting gender compulsion in language in the context of the human preoccupation with gender is not a superficial consideration. We also saw, in the section on Recognition in the previous chapter, that language plays a role in categorizing sexual behaviors. Language plays several influential roles. It is fundamental because language is an often overlooked, yet vital pillar of our society. It is the glue linking generations, enabling skills transfer, communicating traditions, concepts, ideas, methods and beliefs, many of which would otherwise be lost. The way language is structured expresses a fundamental truth about us as a people. For example, until the feminist movement surged forward, language unconsciously (or perhaps by conscious intent of the originators of our languages) communicated a dominant sex. The English language culture used the

---

[17] The Associated Press "When Mark turned Into Maggie" CBS News, February 11, 2009

masculine as the default gender, assigning "he" or "his" to gender neutral discussions. Until feminists emerged, no one needed to be told that it was 'a man's world'. Entrenched culture identified men as the superior sex. That entrenched cultural perspective reigned unquestioned for generation after generation. What appears 'natural' is sometimes learned from the subliminal messages carried through the ages in the language vehicle.

Today, it is politically correct to vary the default gender to give recognition to women in neutral contexts. This is consistent with the social evolution of women in western society through the feminist movement and the quest for equal rights for women beginning around the 1960s. This change in language reflects the social change, demonstrating in a contemporary framework how language reflects culture and promotes and reinforces cultural values. As an example, in the last quarter century, new terns such as "chairperson" were coined to replace the dying tradition "chairman". It is cultural acknowledgement, now embedded in our language, of a new era based on sexual equality.

In using language, one is less aware of the omissions, i.e. what the language does NOT do; for example, the reality that the "his/ her" language construct that became more popular as feminism grew is so far not a his/ her/ other/ construction in popular usage, even as the society begins to acknowledge intersex, transsexual and other sexual identities alongside history's 'men' and 'women'. This 'omission' of any sex other than male or female is a very subtle communication of the society's perceptions that continue in mainstream today. The point here is that our language is not any one person's doing, neither is it wholly the product of a single generation or point in time. Language used speaks silently about what is important to our society and reflects general consensus and formally accepted norms.

This analysis leads to the conclusion that sexual identity is *itself* a message communicated through language. In addition to communicating the intended, overt meaning, language contains subliminal messages about power, culture, values and, not of minimal significance, our sexuality. Our language tradition proclaims that, in our culture, gender is an essential value that must be acknowledged. Language not only indicates the gender and promotes a gender hierarchy, but it also establishes gender as a vital social and cultural element molding the shape of individual identity. Language has an interdependent relationship with society. Whether it is by appropriate vocabulary or subject matter for men and women, the influence of language is so powerful that when we are speaking or listening we are somehow participating in the language dance that helps to choreograph our sexuality.

In this section we have established that language and naming are social elements indelibly molded into our person and serve to define aspects of individual sexual identity. What are other elements of this molded or cultivated identity? Let us unveil other fundamentals of sociosexual identity.

Elements of Cultivated Sexual Identity

... We habitually dismiss traits that are not consistent with the gender expectations of our culture.

Gender-based social acknowledgment prevails throughout the life of an individual. This is demonstrated in a curious masquerade. As part of our tradition, we cultivate and groom a sexual identity to use socially, almost like a strutting peacock displaying a gender spectacle for all to see. Yet, simultaneously, we keep our genitals hidden, always covered. While it is considered vulgar, socially unacceptable, disgraceful, and legally punishable to expose one's genitals in public, we mirror them in a grand social spectacle using everything else that we could find. (One might want to suspect some poorly endowed leader of initiating this tradition of masquerade.) Beyond the naming conventions, this tradition of masquerade is seen in the assignment of roles, behaviors, grooming, hairstyles, lipsticks, jobs, salaries, rewards, expectations, even attitudes dominating our social lives based on sexual differences. We flirt and flash our sexual endowment using external accessories. In effect, we flaunt a fake representation of sexuality. Because of this, socially acknowledged gender clues need not directly mirror any biological reality, yet people rely on them to perceive gender socially.

Another carefully cultivated element is the sexual image that we project socially. Faithful to the tradition of masquerade, we each assume and project some *social* image, all the time keeping our genitals covered. We similarly dress and undress, groom and shape this identity. Grooming establishes not just a social identity, but reflects *rules* of gender-based identity that society has established over several millennia and which have become embedded in its fabric. We *all* learn to display and project in a limitless kaleidoscope of gender identity factors for others to see, *instead of* underlying gender. That limitless kaleidoscope helps to translate gender into a sexual identity.

Rules dominate the cultivation of sexual identity. In the first chapter, we defined the character of our culture as a 'culture of straights'; a culture that has historically set the tone for our perception of reality and our social systems based on an assumption of gender and a presumption of heterosexuality. From the moment of birth our culture begins to entrench and emphasize sexual distinctions. Throughout the western world sexual separation is established. There are rules governing separate behaviors of men and women, roles in the home, and traditions governing employment practices among others.

Sexual hierarchy

In addition to helping us perceive gender, social values also convey a gender hierarchy. In this hierarchy, men are the dominant sex, women are the dependent sex and any other sex is perceived as beneath those two. We convey those values in a measurable way in the accumulation of money and possessions. Money and possessions not only reflect a financial hierarchy, but also follow the gender hierarchy. One example of this is that today men continue to earn more than women in the working environment. This was confirmed in a recent salary analysis published by CNN Money Magazine[18] entitled "The 76-cent myth". This shows how social processes help to cultivate the sexual hierarchy. The dominant sex *is* the dominant paycheck. In this way, the traditional glass ceiling establishes and maintains a sexual hierarchy using money and power—men at the top, women under the ceiling. Similarly, roles and behaviors and the cloaks and feathers in which we shroud and display ourselves carry messages to others and reflect unspoken messages we want to convey.

In today's society, sexuality, the sexual appeal or awareness of an individual, is also associated with a financial hierarchy. Evidence of this is seen in the media, particularly in media advertising. Wealth and glamour are frequently portrayed as "sexy". Further, there are those who habitually use wealth and possessions to make sexual advances. This supports the argument that in our society what is considered sexy can be something other than physical. Not only can wealth be an operative concern in sexual relationships, it is a historical fact that sexual favors are traded (illegally in most societies) for money. Prostitution is an illustration of the capacity of the human being to be driven by financial considerations to make sexual alliances. This is not to say that wealth or poverty determine sexuality, nor that financial considerations are present in all sexual alliances. The goal here is understanding human capacity and uncovering the spectrum of different factors present in sexual connections. Individual choice in the use or development of any factor is not denied. This talk about money is also not a judgmental discourse. The evidence of money and financial

---

[18] Sahadi, Jeanne, "The 76-cent myth", CNN Money, Feb 21, 2006

consideration as an operative factor in some sexual alliances supports the position that social value is one dimension operative in such alliances.

The reality that a prostitute may be driven by other basic needs—the effects of poverty, hunger, survival instincts—enhance the argument that sexual alliance in our society has the likeness of a commodity. We are not helpless slaves to a mystical urge. Individuals assert choice and are known to trade sexual alliances in different circumstances.

Sociosexual rules govern and maintain these distinctions. For the various rules to work there must be conformity. Conformity in this sense is not consensus. Conformity is accomplished by systems of acceptance and rejection, while consensus implies some form of agreement. Vocal protests reported in the media against the status quo in this century, reflect disagreement. More subtly, the gay movement, understandably labeled an "alternative" lifestyle, is also evidence of formal challenge to sociosexual traditions. The label itself is implicit of the dominance of heterosexuality. The implication appears to be that, despite the expanded list of gender types, identities and orientation practices, the conventional sexual culture is not inherently diverse. When there is genuine acceptance of diversity, pejorative and alienating labels would fade into disuse and lose potency.

Acceptance, defined as the popular reception as a valid member of the social group in which one participates, is another element of socially cultivated sexual identity. There are different degrees of acceptance that may be regarded on a continuum that extends from full acceptance to rejection. Sharing responsibility for accepting or rejecting an identity, the social group (our society) collectively maintains the cultivation of sexual identity.

Masquerading sexual image, rules and practices enforcing them, conformity and establishment of states deemed 'natural' and 'normal' are just some of the ways that sexual identity is nurtured and cultivated. These in turn perpetuate value systems. This is consistent with Edward Wilson's theory previously cited, about the connection between gender and the environment: that one's identity is essentially the cultural environment interacting with genes.

Other elements that reflect gender include elements of dress, attitude and style. These frame the observed biology and the attached gender and reflect a cultural practice, a social 'handle' cultivated in kaleidoscope as 'normal' sexual identity.

Evidence that the visual observation of gender takes precedence over other biological markers of gender rests in the way amniocentesis is used. One of the findings from amniocentesis performed on expectant mothers is the sex of her unborn baby. In this process, doctors analyze samples of amniotic fluid extracted from the mother. Occasionally, when the baby is born, the sex is not that expected based on the analysis of amniotic fluid. The way this is handled is very revealing about what takes precedence. In this situation, the fluid analysis, not the genitals, is considered to be in error. This is a clear statement of the rule that the visual markers take precedence over other clues that may be currently available.

This illustration may be interpreted to mean that according to tradition, not genes, not science, but genitals are the primary cultural clue to sexual identity.   Genitals take precedence over any contradictory scientific, social or other test. In our minds, no other test surpasses that. If it did, we would uphold the findings of the amniotic fluid over the presence of the genitals.   In the same manner that we dismiss the amniocentesis, we habitually dismiss traits that are not consistent with the gender expectations of our culture.   Governed by tradition, this tunnel vision that from birth one's genitals are the key to one's sexual identity is an important factor in how society recognizes elements of our sexuality. As Helen Boyd's account about her cross-dressing husband concluded:

> *there are no "traits" inherent in either gender, but rather that we all have different aptitudes and proclivities, some of which are encouraged if we are women, discouraged if we are men.*[19]

To extend Helen Boyd's perception, there may be as many human varieties as there are rose bushes, but cultural practices, including performing surgery on the rare intersex child, maintain the conventional gender dichotomy.   In contrast, we treasure the rarest roses and seek to cultivate more of the rarest ones. As individuals and groups we are all part of the maintenance system enforcing values; monitoring not the biology, but the symbols—the names, the clothing, the hair, decorated or plain finger nails—the kaleidoscope that we cultivate. We recognize, acknowledge and re-affirm these social representations of sexual identity that we nurture ourselves. It is a self-sustaining process. Starting early in our lives the process re-enforces the external demarcating gender lines in the culture and attempts to cultivate a very particular socialization beginning from the cradle. It is true that there is the opportunity for choice. A mother may choose to dress her boy in pink dresses. However, this rarely, if ever happens. This process is so much part of the unconscious that cultivating elements of gender is accepted as 'natural'. The symbols all *speak for* the gender. This is consistent with what Wilson defined as individuals molded by interaction of environment, especially cultural environment, with original genetics. Like a closed system, it establishes a norm that ensures that the variables of behavior and treatment become welded to fixed genitalia.

While our genitals are not variable, (at least not without intervention) this constant merging of the social and the sexual person, consistent with the framework detected by scientists as the molding of environment and genes, forms an agile *sociosexual* identity. It is not a static part of our selves. It grows with us, being shaped and pruned first by our parents and guardians, then by ourselves and anyone we encounter by established norms and standards of 'natural' behavior that evolve to represent perspectives. We chisel and mold, groom, disrobe and repackage our identities to match perspectives of nature. In the process, the growing individual would 'find' the image that best reflects their perspective of themselves. In this sense, the process leading to maturity based on norms external to one's biological self is a cultural practice, a *pseudo*-sexual development that occurs parallel to whatever biological changes occur.

---

[19] Boyd, Helen, *My Husband Betty*, Thunder's Mouth Press, New York, 2003, p 45

Unlike coming of age, maturing into adulthood, graduating, retirement, and the like, there is no fixed final stage in the evolution of one's sociosexual identity. It is not a static, objective reality. Instead, it is personal, subject to the individual circumstance. As evidenced by recent upsurges in protests against rules, such as military and marital practices (discussed in Chapter 6: Law, Policy and Rights), some people are comfortable with who they are and the governing rules and their roles in society, while others are not. It is for those who are not, that identity could become frustrating. However, one may ask, is it the comfort level or the identity itself that creates the frustration? If the rules were reversed, would people who are now comfortable with their roles become uncomfortable and vice versa?

It is the rules and our peace with conformance or nonconformance, not identity itself, that is the source of the dissonance. As evidence of this, one may cite the array of new gender identities that have emerged since Webster last defined gender as essentially a dichotomy. One may also cite quietly cross-dressing heterosexuals whose habits of dress deliberately conform to an opposite gender.

This suggests that we differ not by our roles but by the social and cultural *rules* of exclusion and acceptance. The sex detected by our genitalia may be a biological constant but *what it means to us*, our sociosexual identity, is a social dynamic. The sociosexual identity can be as volatile, dynamic and elastic as the images one can perceive in society.

So far, we have identified language, modes of dress and naming as western society's first approaches to separating and distinguishing the sexes. We have also identified the concept of the masquerade, sexual image and its representation in society and the extent to which norms are established so that what is natural is essentially some perspective of a relationship between nature and society. Sociosexual elements are vital, not because they affect or change gender, but because they create certainty in the socialization process.

One may conclude from all this that the truism that human beings are gregarious animals is a fundamental aspect of human sexual development. Our sexuality, like our humanity, is about *being*. We are not merely biological cells hostage to cellularity. Could you imagine an animal with a wild head of hair, long, unkempt finger and toenails, grunting incomprehensively as he tramples a field of rare cigar orchids in recreational hunting of the endangered Irish red deer with no rules to guide him? Instead we learn to speak, trim our hair and nails, shave our legs, make and wear clothes and love and care for each other and for other species. In essence, we *learn* how to be, and in *being* acquire identity. To develop this discussion, an examination of the processes that serve to maintain the elements of cultivated sexual identity is necessary.

Nurturing and Controlling Sociosexual Identity

...Sociosexual identity is nurtured via the sexual associations of social accessories

As children grow, other codes are added to distinguish sexual identity. While we identify young babies by color codes in clothing, we identify young children by different styles of clothing and hair and to a lesser extent clothing color. To these are added attitudes and activities, learned behaviors and grooming as the child gets older. More rules increasingly enhance and nurture this identity as we teach the little mites and prepare them for more coding and expectations throughout their lives; a different set for boys and a different set for girls, as for example, the selection of toys and games for boys and girls, recreational activities, recommendations for educational subject matter, the award of social permissions and freedoms, schooling in decorum, as well as the assignment of familial responsibilities for growing boys and girls. As they become adults, social coding and expectations become absorbed into their sexual identities. External attributes, which have no relation to sexual biology, can in this way become intermixed with later doubts (or certainties) and feelings in general about their identity.

This sociosexual identity is nurtured by consensus as to the sexual associations of certain social accessories. It is not an intrinsic identity, but more of an assumed cloak intended to *project* the identity and for many today has come to *represent* an identity itself. This may be considered to be a necessary function of the social organization of our sexes.

That is to say, in the same manner that a judge is immediately recognized in the courtroom or a priest in the church, because of their professional attire, so too are men and women recognized in organized society.

Organization is, however, just stage setting. Once organized into the distinct gender and identity camps, the stage is set for further social orientation and development. Other social processes follow through. Society nurtures these "cloaks", these identity badges, so consistently that it often mistakenly uses them as if they were the identity. I have heard a mother assert that she knew that her infant son wanted to be a girl when as a toddler he kept demanding the pink kid's cup (sippy cup) like his twin sister, while she kept insisting on the blue one. Another saw her son's insistence on wearing dresses as a signal about his gender. We need to ask ourselves what wearing a dress or preferring pink has to do with sexuality, especially in a child who displays no overt sexual interest and perhaps will not do so for a dozen years? This is the social imprint on gender and on sexual identity.

Historically, the entrenched social rules are inflexible and intolerant of individual preferences. The rules and norms established for the particular gender label given to an individual must be adhered to. They are recognized and supported by traditions. For example, beyond the traditions of the crib and dressing in pink and blue, there are traditions of behavior for boys and girls, traditions of grooming and traditions of learning and education that parents, schools, associations and employers follow. As soon as an individual steps out of the traditional mold, that individual's sexual identity is often questioned by society.

In addition to nurturing through entrenched traditions, we also nurture the sexes by distinct standards of female beauty and masculinity. Society routinely establishes aspirations through beauty contests, glamour magazines for young women, or muscle building contests with opposing 'beauty' standards aimed at young men. These work because we are social beings with an instinct or habit of socializing. We share and hand down our aspirations. As those standards change, so too do our aspirations. As an example, consider the evolution of the Miss America contest to include talent and educational aspirations. That evolution parallels changes in the value society placed on women through active contest years, including changes in the formal education for women influenced by the feminist movement. These practices of differentiating the sexes and encouraging different values and standards for each are part of the social and cultural nurturing. It is a strategy of positive reinforcement of the standards.

There is both positive and negative reinforcement of sociosexual standards. Society also controls behaviors by violence, punishment and penalties for non-conformance. In the case of gender, identity and orientation, one price of non-conformance has been social rejection and ridicule. Although there is a climate of change, even today extreme behaviors are found and sadly, individuals who do not conform may pay with their lives at the hands of other individuals.

The gay riots of the sixties and the sporadic violence against gays today testify to that. Mark Thompson, in his documentary *Long Road to Freedom: The Advocate History of the Gay and Lesbian Movement,* described the Stonewall riots of 1969, and how the official (police) treatment of gays was aggressive and harassing.[20]   The threat of aggression puts fear and defensiveness in the picture. The opposite is also true. Individuals who may want to be regarded as the opposite gender and refuse to follow social norms can equally demonstrate anger, aggression and violence toward themselves or to those who refuse to acknowledge them as anything other than they desire. It is important to recognize these guardians. Violence, hatred and fear, whether self-inflicted or imposed, reflect the level of acceptability and tolerance in society.

More recently, in 1995, the incident dubbed the 'Talk Show Murder' provided an extreme example of violence associated with sexual identity. A guest on a television program selected a beautifully dressed woman who turned out to be a transvestite man.   The guest's response moved from embarrassment to murder. The response suggests to me that he could not accept his attraction to someone other than a woman. One may conclude that his response to sociosexual stimuli– to clothing and style marred his self image and sexual identity. This analysis suggests that he could not separate his lifelong indoctrination in male and female "codes" and his habits of attraction from his definition of sexuality.   Not understanding sociosexual phenomena and recognizing the transience of sociosexual identity may have been the ultimate faux pas for this man: A mistake that challenged the core of his sexual identity and his sexual behavior. It would seem that he felt compelled to retaliate and that although he was attracted to this beautiful

---

[20] Thompson, Mark, *Long Road to Freedom*, The Advocate, Los Angeles, 1994, p.28

looking person, he did not _want to be_ attracted to a man. He was tricked because this man wore the wrong codes. Because he was attracted to that man dressed in woman's codes, it did not mean that he was attracted to men. Unable to express this in words, his violent reaction may be seen as the zealous protest of a guardian of the codes. This story is significant not only for its demonstration of how seriously guarding the cultivated codes is regarded, but also for the opportunity to observe our complete immersion in the codes and to distinguish it from sexuality. Hopefully, being more conscious of the sociosexual stimuli can relieve the dissonance and tension some people feel about the traditions of our society.

Many theories have been proposed to explain these responses. Most persuasively is Peter Corning's proposition about synergy. Corning argues that our cultural evolution is "a cumulative cultural inheritance that each new generation builds upon."[21] In other words we commit to the traditions we inherit.

Cultivated, nurtured and controlled elements do not portray the whole identity. Other dimensions, such as hormones, genes and DNA, which are not socially cultivated, may play essential roles in sexual identity. Is the society or the biology the driving force? Wilson proposes that we simply do not know which aspects of our nature and/ or our environment shape us.

---

[21] Corning, Peter, _Nature's Magic_, Cambridge University Press, Cambridge, 2003, p.277

Gender Based Behavior as Sociosexual Phenomena

...We cultivate other social classes and give them gender labels hardly even recognizing that this is what we are doing

We have discussed how clothing and dress become the marks of sexual identity independently of the identity itself. In turn, how people behave or respond to these marks of sexual identity are interpreted as statements of their sexual identity. For example, in western society, boys who prefer frills and girls who prefer not to use make up, become concerned about their sexual identity, *not about their preferences in clothing.* Parents begin to deduce transgender signals based on a child's taste in clothing, toys and attitudes. In evaluating the bases of the child's choice (preference in hair styling and clothing), one recognizes social choices and a social statement. Because our culture fails to separate social identity from sexual identity, children making a social statement may be seen as declaring a sexual preference. In other words, our culture not only wants women to don women's garb, but also pushes those (or the guardians of those) preferring women's roles to understand this as a sexual statement: equating "I want to wear lipstick" with "I want to be a woman". For example, in 2012, an mnsbc.com report[22] on a program documenting the experiences of transgender children seeking and obtaining medical help, quoted statistics from the Children's Hospital in Boston about a quadruple increase in the number of children reportedly seeking this type of medical help. It can

---

[22] http://insidedateline.msnbc.com, "Transgender Children in America encounter new crossroads with medicine.", July 8, 2012

be expected that this number may continue to increase as the various identity options become known, *unless society stops trying to pigeon hole people sexually* That is one method we use to nurture and control sociosexual identity.

The rules of social behavior set apart, for example, men who want to wear lipstick from those that have been turned from dressing up and categorize only one behavior as male. These social standards or behaviors connote sexual distinctions in our culture. In this sense, they (both the rules and the behaviors) may be considered to be *socio*sexual phenomena.

An individual's sociosexual identity holds such a strong position that discomfort or dissatisfaction with expected roles, attitudes, and partnerships may create problems for that person. That may explain the report carried in msnbc.com about gender identity disorders (GID) in children, documenting an increase in psychological problems in relation to gender identity in children[23]. This mirrors the increase in public awareness and discussion about a wider spectrum of gender identities. Like an incredible hulk, the expectations take on a life of their own and become master of the identity. People who do not conform or share the expectations may feel varying forms of dissatisfaction, or unease. As a society, our thinking makes us create new classes based on the social trappings we ourselves create, and shift the non-conformers into these classes and define them with different labels. In other words, we create new gender clusters beyond the initial male

---

[23] http://vitals.msnbc.msn.com, "More transgender kids getting help, seeking treatment". Feb 2, 2012

and female based on social conformity or non-conformity. This urge is equally pressing on all sides of the spectrum of conformity. It is interesting that the labeling and identifying often come from the groups themselves. They emerge as sociosexual phenomena: people *want* their sexual identity to be seen and acknowledged socially. Perhaps it is a necessity in order to recognize and meet like-minded individuals. The need to define people, including ourselves, based on these essentially socially assigned and acquired traits, is cultural. It becomes a circular process so that when the definition does not fit perfectly, rules exert pressure to force individuals to conform. Evidence of extreme pressure is reflected in medically administered solutions such as the administration of hormones, "blockers" that suppress puberty, surgery and therapy. The pressure to conform is deep seated. Individuals express feeling trapped, not by the social systems, but by their bodies. People want to look and dress and behave in a certain manner. They want to conform to the system. For example, this was expressed in the aforementioned case of Mark who became Maggie, and who felt that his body was "uncomfortable". Social and sexual identity are so well fused in our culture that individuals may reject themselves as they reach for the sociosexual expectations.

We live in a society aware today of homosexuals, heterosexuals and many other sex-based categories or classes of people. So far, the argument about sociosexual phenomena is that we start with gender, use various codes (behaviors, activities etc.) to represent them socially while the differentiating biology remains hidden, then in a circular process, society turns around and takes the codes to tell us what the sexes are, or use surgical or other methods to align the biology with the preferred codes. When it comes to sexual partnerships, the question is this: is it the social behavior that forms the basis of these categorizations, or is it some intrinsic component? In the social context it is more the behavior, including individual declaration, which serves to distinguish people and facilitate categorizations.

How do the categories emerge? It is not that behaviors are new. An examination of social networking websites reveals search options that are traditional, men seeking women, women seeking men; men seeking men and women seeking women. Yet, we as a society define additional groups and create new terminology and give recognition to an array of new clusters. In essence, we end up with the traditional clusters identified above, and an array of sociosexual clusters that differentiate themselves by a kaleidoscope of social and sexual factors. [It is understood that categories for these other clusters may perhaps be missing from the search options because they socialize in different Internet communities, and that more categories would be added over time] These clusters and definitions are created not by a defined biology, but by our society's attempt to label and categorize different groups of people. Terms such as SGL (Same Gender Loving) may be relatively new, but is there something fundamentally different about people who use this label? We have not examined the role of genes, hormones and DNA. A brief overview of those dimensions is pursued in Chapter 3: Anatomy and Identity. With regard to social phenomena we need to acknowledge that the definitions and the array of categorizations are born of the differences or similarities in the way people conform to social expectations.

Transvestite behavior among heterosexuals confirms that dress preferences, though they may violate our social definitions of sexuality, nevertheless need not reflect innate sexuality. As Helen Boyd points out in her insightful writing about her husband who is a transvestite[24], cross dressers are often heterosexual. Their dress, not their sexuality is non-conforming. This is consistent with the perspective that the styling orientation and dress sense begun in the cradle are social directions based on visible genitalia. Scottish kilts and Indian Saris, Englishman's bowler hats and West African woman's turbans, along with miniskirts, skorts and skirts, painted toe nails, earrings and high heeled shoes relate to gender, not because of some microbiological proclivity, but because the particular society makes it so. In this sense, transvestite behavior may be seen as a social phenomenon displaying our markers of sexual identity in its own form without attachment to the sexual identity norm. In that sense it can be recognized not as sexual but a cultural behavior.

The term transgender is frequently used to describe a person who does not conform to what we define as the *social* style and attitude of a particular gender. In a series of profiles aired on Abcnews in April and May 2007[25], the term was applied to children who were not conforming to the expectations we set for a child of a particular gender. It was not as we often apply it, a statement of sexuality or gender, but of the *social identity of our recognized sexual classes.*

---

[24] Boyd, Helen, *op. cit.* p. 11
[25] Walters, Barbara, "My Secret Self: A Story of Transgender Children", abcnews, April 27 2007

The narrative compared behavior and the expected behavior in children who had not reached the age of sexual maturity, and made conclusions and categorizations about gender. Perspectives that the child had a disorder and a birth defect were shared as conclusions.

An understanding of the phenomenon of sociosexual identity may be of value in our responses to children, particularly where there are no sexual developments to speak of. Because we generally internalize the sociosexual rules, we as adults may read sexual overtones into the behaviors of children with regard to these rules. Adults bred with pink/ blue, skirt/ pants, doll/ truck cultural expectations may interpret the behavior of children using these social markers as gender indicators, preventing their sons from wearing dresses. As members of the culture of straights, they feel it is their duty. It will be useful to further study the sociosexual aspect of the transgender description. Further research contrasting American, Scottish, British, West African, Indian and diverse cultural gender expectations could serve to distinguish the social trappings in our sexual and gender labels. When we look at children it may be useful to withhold judgments about sexuality based on displays of social and behavioral independence from or preferences inconsistent with established expectations and fashions.

This may seem confusing, but the rudiments of our definitions separate biology from identity. It is our culture that loads outer trappings and social expectations onto that biology. It is our culture and our value systems that govern the rules and behavior, separating them into categories of acceptability and unacceptability.

Every person is different and hence every relationship. Some gay couples dress according to heterosexual roles, one in traditional male clothing and the other in traditional female clothing. 'Who wears the pants' becomes more than an idiom. Instead, short hair and gents clothing, long hair, lipstick, high heels and ladies cologne are cultivated and become intermixed in the sexual role differentiation in the relationship. It is an interesting observation that suggests that, although in homosexual relationships the heterosexual traditions are rejected, the traditional roles themselves and cultural trappings need not be.

The Betty Boyd studies previously referred to provide new insights into this. The studies suggest that dress is not a statement of sexuality. The studies encourage us to conclude that our thinking is so entrenched that when it comes to gender-based behavior, social codes (for example attraction to and love for lipstick and high heels) may be mistaken as biological flare. Non-conformity may mistakenly raise sexual doubt, trigger sexual frustration and uncertainty and may unnecessarily prompt sexual identity crises.

Institutionalized Sociosexual Codes

> *...Institutions shape what we become and how acceptable it is.*

Of course, the social dimension is only one dimension of our sexuality, the most visible one. This sociosexual imprint manifests itself on a daily basis as we interact with each other. It is perceived largely through visual and behavioral clues. There is no question whatever, that if you dress as a man, you are treated as a man, wear women's clothing and you are mistaken for a woman. Unlike the other dimensions, this sociosexual dimension requires collaborative, complicit maintenance. This discussion asserts that this maintenance is accomplished partly through institutions.

Although the social codes are mostly "removable" (i.e. individuals can cut and style their hair and eyebrows, change fashions, shave, remove or wear makeup etc.), rules are deeply entrenched. As previously demonstrated, people guard them with an abiding passion. Institutions and groups also play a significant role in maintaining the traditions. In discussing the acceleration and retardation of progress, Gordon Childe in his book *"Man Makes Himself"* describes tradition as created and transmitted by people but nevertheless changeable.[26] He argues:

> *tradition makes the man by circumscribing his behavior within certain bounds; but it is equally true that man makes the traditions. And so, we can repeat with deeper insight, 'Man makes himself'.*

---

[26] Childe, Gordon, *op. cit.* p. 188

This concept does not refer to individual man. People form different subgroups that promote and re-enforce particular views and understandings among their members. These groups may be families, churches, mosques, synagogues, schools, gangs, clubs, teams, neighborhoods, towns, cities, states, countries, races... the definitions are limitless. For example, churches follow established commandments; businesses develop mission, policy and disciplinary statements; teams develop rules and penalties; gangs have rites; states develop laws; schools teach rules and behaviors; and families nurture character and behavioral traits. The point is that institutions are part of how and what we learn and become and believe to be truth.

Institutions create formal rules and formalize standards of behaviors, including gender identity and orientation standards. Informal society, in contrast, often passes on unspoken rules as tradition through observation, ceremony and practice. Together, formal and informal society determine how we are educated and what we are taught. It will not be true to say that they *determine* what we become in an overt manner. More accurately, as guardians, they influence what we perceive, preserve the status quo and the agenda up for consideration, thus shaping what we become and views concerning how acceptable it is.

The processes used by institutions vary, but evidence shows similarities in the processes. Many of the institutions listed have written rules governing sexual behaviors, but not all rules are written. As an example, a New York congressman who sent a photograph of his crotch clothed in underpants, ultimately resigned from congress because this was found out. Not only is it significant that the incident became a news-worthy item, but also that it was reported that his colleagues sought to prompt him to resign and that the President of the United States considered him an embarrassment[27]. Once written, members pledge allegiance either through signature or through spoken pledge. Once pledged, tactics of enforcement include repetition in slogans, teaching and preaching. Penalties for non-conformity serve to control behavior. These include suspensions, fines, ridicule, ostracism and dismissal and self imposed penalties such as resignation from office.

Behaviors are in these ways institutionalized within the particular groups. Nevertheless, given freedom of association, membership is optional. It is therefore true that (except for national laws that apply to everyone), individuals do not have to subscribe to required behaviors. Only *member* behavior is regulated. Further, some informal groups and anti-social groups develop illegal rules and practices that violate personal freedom. These include gang rites and hate crimes.

Establishment of rules is not a conclusive determinant of behavior. Individuals can just as easily respond differently to any laws, creeds and tradition and fear tactics. Observation shows responses to institutionalized roles ranging from adherence, hidden or closet behaviors, combined with public displays of adherence, and open rejection.

---

[27] HuffingtonPost.com, "Anthony Weiner Resigns", July 14, 2011,

Whether we agree with Corning that we commit to the traditions we inherit, or with Childe that we make ourselves, or with any other theorist, is a personal judgment. Yet, the evidence shows that individuals and groups of people guard sociosexual traditions and culture with teaching, regulation, passion, commitment, fear, penalties and even illegal practices and violence.

Sociosexual Attraction

Sexual attraction could be inspired by the social codes and our interpretation of them

Differentiating between social, sexual and sociosexual phenomena may help clarify the rudiments of human yearnings and desires. In this regard, it may be helpful to examine attraction more closely. Attraction may be described as the 'pull' factor that makes us interested in something or someone. Often, attraction is presumed to be sexual. The term 'sexual attraction' is going to be used here only for an attraction that has a sexual purpose or reaction. Because the sexes are defined, identified and recognized using many social codes as shown above, an initial attraction to someone could be intertwined with the customary codes. To begin this discussion, we may argue that in a social setting even when there is a sexual intent or reaction, sexual attraction could be inspired by the social codes and our interpretation of them, becoming by synthesis a sociosexual attraction.

Recalling the case of Schmitz in the "Talk Show Murder" incident previously referred to, we can begin to understand the interplay between attraction and sexual behavior. In the processes previously described our social identity is fused with biological identity. What we recognize and respond to is therefore a complex kaleidoscope, including traditions of grooming and style fused with the individual self.

Other clarity is provided in the case "When Mark became Maggie" previously referred to. One interpretation is that Mark changed appearances to resolve a dissonance between what was felt, and the social expression of those feelings. That transformation included both hormone therapy and psychological therapy. There was also specific help to get dressed as Maggie. These steps encapsulate the elements that form the whole individual who then becomes the subject or object of attraction.

Taking the two cases together, one can gage that Schmitz was responding not to some biological gender, but to a sociosexual identity. Schmitz sensitivity mirrors the cultural perception that sexuality is biology. The findings presented here suggest that it is not and that sexuality may never have been a mirror of biology. In civil settings, sexual identity is for all of us an interpretation and grooming to represent and display assigned or desired gender. Feelings though they originate internally, are responses to external stimuli that are the result of interpretation and grooming.

Clearly, attraction is not as simple as clothing and what we wear. However, one does hear assertions that make it seem that way, such as: "From as far back as I could remember I've always wanted to wear lipstick" and "I knew I was gay

from the time I was a child because I didn't want to wear..."
this or wear that, play with this or play with that.
Recognizing sociosexual phenomena is an important step to
understanding our sexuality.

As demonstrated, attraction that first occurs in person is
often visual. As individuals get closer to each other, other
more fundamental characteristics become revealed. Each
stage of interaction reveals more and uncovers deeper bases
to sustain or demolish attraction.

As attraction in persons is often visual, attraction over the
Internet is firstly through the medium of text. In a culture
where it has historically been believed that we interact with
each other as biological beings, the reality and power of
Internet attraction may appear novel. However, given the
findings presented above, social individuals have always been
representing and projecting a sexual image. The Internet is
merely a change in medium. In addition, the Internet also
offers means of projecting the image through photographic
and video imagery.

Before the advent of the Internet, people maintained long
distance relationships through letter writing and later the
telephone. Pen pals fell in love and entered into lasting
relationships. Again, the pen was just another medium for
representing and projecting images of self. Telephone sex is
another example where sexual outcomes, such as orgasms,
are accomplished without any physical or visual contact.
Instead, the ear is the organ of sexual "contact", and the
brain translates the words or sounds into a sexual message–
an intellectual activity.

These disparate cases suggest that attraction, although originating intrinsically, is a response to a projected, representative person, not necessarily a biological mass. It occurs through the brain's translation of received stimuli. In order to reveal our intrinsic nature it may be helpful to peel back the layers of these assertions to see where biology ends and social customs begin.

CHAPTER 3: ANATOMY AND IDENTITY

To humans are born two different babies.

The only visible physical difference observable between a boy and a girl at birth is often their sex organs. We discussed in the preceding chapters how that observable difference is assigned gender. It is not that there are no other differences, but the label of boy or girl hinges on the sex organs and that is the definitive feature of the anatomy that is visible at birth. Although studies of hormones, genes, DNA and other biology reveal differences, these considerations are not currently part of that initial investigation that determines or even influences the documentation and announcement of a newborn's gender.

The Voice of Sexual Identity

As adults, when we consider our identity, some of the features we want or don't want are choices based on our consciousness. Others are not dependent on individual selection and conscious behavior. But the difference often emerges subtly. Learned behavior could be so subtle that we could be left feeling that we were born with what we learn. For example, most of us can distinguish between the voice of a child and that of an adult, between a man's voice and that of a woman. Often, there is something about an old woman's voice or an old man's voice that tells us without seeing them, that the person is old. Although we would mostly be correct in our identification, we would find it very difficult to explain to someone exactly how we knew. A lot of that difficulty is because our language does not have the precise vocabulary for us to define all the nuances of voice. Similarly, we can recognize a particular person without seeing them, but if you were asked to describe the voice and precisely explain how you are able to identify the owner, that would be tough to do. The skill is however imprecise. At times, a keen listener may hear a voice that is neither wholly male nor wholly female, though that need not be a reflection of the person's gender. Again, a constraint of linguistics and of our training and acuity.

The point is that voice, although it is a factor in sexual differentiation, remains unexplored. By extension, the role it plays in adult sexual identity and social interaction is acknowledged but not explored nor understood.

Cultivated Identity in Hair

Hair is a reality. Some of us have more than others. To begin with, we have no control over where hair grows on our bodies but we groom and nurture our hair. Our culture uses hair to define us, and in so doing helps to shape our perception and response to the presence of hair in ourselves and in others. For example, both males and females tend to have hair on their heads from birth. We also know that as the individual biology develops into adulthood both grow pubic hair and continue to grow hair on their heads. We also observe that hair grows more profusely on the face, chest, arms, legs and back of men but in general women have no hair in these parts of the body. These may seem trite observations but are cited here as observable evidence of difference consistent with the original observation of gender difference.

Features observed at birth are aspects of biology. However, whatever sex we identify with as we develop and grow usually determines how we handle this biological growth and what we do about it. Those actions are cultural. Nevertheless hair presence itself is a biological statement; one that we may or may not be happy about, but nevertheless is an assertion of our biology. Shaving or not shaving one's hair may make a social statement, but it does not change that biology. As a society, we have cultivated different gender attitudes to hair, but as individuals our grooming is a choice based on where we see ourselves. That perception also determines whether other intervention or action is 'necessary'. Drugs, hormones, treatments, therapies or other techniques support, encourage or change hair growth to affect how we are seen and to change the *perception* of our biology. For example, in the previously mentioned case when Mark became Maggie, hormones were used to control hair growth so that it would be aligned with that expected of a woman.

Muscle– Sociosexual Cause or Effect?

One can hardly discuss noticeable physical differences between men and women without pointing to muscular development. This is where the discussion gets a bit more complicated. It is difficult to determine exactly how much of the muscularity evident in men is due to culture and social habits that have over time cultivated a softer sex and a more muscular one. We learn from the body building sport how much more predisposed mens' bodies are to muscle building. A man and a woman starting at the same apparent level of muscularity and exercising approximately the same amount of time, would not see the same level of muscle development and the same rate of muscle increase.

However that is descriptive of the status quo. What is understated is that culturally women have not been encouraged into bodybuilding. The cultural evidence is that female bodybuilding is in its relative infancy as a sport and traditional society still discourages women from pursuing muscularity. Even more persuasive is the preponderance of grown mature men still pursuing opportunities in competitive and professional sport, activities which build and exercise muscle. In other terms, our practices may be held responsible for systematically cultivating male muscle and strength. Comparatively, there are fewer opportunities for and examples of mature women in active professional sport.

Many may want to pursue this discussion about whether muscle is indeed a physical distinction or organs encouraged or evolved by the historic consistency of our system of *treating* the sexes, as well as systems of encouragement and assigning social roles. Systems of encouragement include the award of prizes and the criteria used in the award of those prizes, particularly for body building contests, and beauty contests. Although this discussion is peripheral, it is recognized that systems of encouragement could have a more profound effect.

The central point is that physical differentiation between the male and female human body may be visually perceived, but it is also deliberately cultivated. We recognize biology because of its physical reminders. However, cultural practices enhance and exaggerate the basic differences. Human biology is not the untouched orchid in the depths of an unexplored jungle. Our biology is touched by our culture. Barbara Katz Rothman's book *Genetic Maps and Human Imaginations*[vi] makes the point that a person does not just mature independently. Even babies, though fed and kept warm, die if they are not nurtured.[28] If we accept that human biology does not thrive only by sustaining biology, we can hardly regard our biology as the jury of a life sentence; or deem human sexuality to be entirely a biological reality.

Revelation's "Bingo" and Biology

This is by no means a proposition that hair, muscle and voice make us what we are. Not at all. It is an assertion of layers of individual identity. Biology is merely one layer of

---

[28] Rothman, Barbara Katz, *Genetic Maps and Human Imagination*, W.W Norman & Co. Inc., New York, 1998, p. 226

self. The point is, various biological changes happen whether we want them to or not. Our biology is revealed to us as we grow. These biological features are not choices of our consciousness. Our consciousness is just that recognition, that "bingo" moment, when we realize who we are. I remember a young man telling me how terrified he felt when he first saw pubic hair on his body. No one had told him that that would happen; he had never seen it on anyone and he felt horrified, afraid and dirty. A freak with a secret he tried desperately to hide and remove. This is an amusing illustration about response to the gifts of biology. It is how we respond to the prize and what we do with the prize that is our gift to ourselves and to the rest of the world.

The experience of the little boy is also an example of expectation and acceptance. The boy was unprepared for the changes in his body and rejected them.

Among other things, our response includes socially cultivated subconscious beliefs, thoughts and ideas as much as it includes our attitude to how society shapes and cultivates our thinking. I am not saying that it is exclusively comprised of our social subconscious. The point is that the social subconscious (or even our social consciousness) can be seen in some of our responses to our bodies. In the same way that we shout "bingo" when our cards match in a bingo game, we declare our sexuality in response to the available offerings and expectations we are made aware of as we socialize, learn or are educated.

Genes, hormones and DNA

Although these biological identifiers are not included in defining the social imprint that pervades our sexual identity and orientation, the recognition of sociosexual elements may be important to progress by scientists defining genes and DNA of sexuality. Over the years, various researchers and scientists have pursued the biology of human sexuality under a microscope and in laboratories. In their search for the gay gene, Hamer and Copeland[29] were not able to find a conclusive genetic indicator of sexuality. However one could see many sociosexual elements in the sample. This means that the sample population itself may have included a mix of individuals who, although all admitting a common identity, may have diverse sociosexual qualifiers. More vividly for example, let us say a sample population of one legged men was being studied to find the gene responsible for a condition called oneleggedism. Researchers would need to separate those whose leg condition was natal from those who developed the condition through some social or other process—an accident, war, and a myriad of other possibilities. So too, without having an open mind about the influences on human sexuality, genetic research could be confused by sample populations that do not acknowledge the presence of both genetic predispositions and social influences on individual development. Some may have been genetically inspired while others may have been created by society, recalling Wilson's discussion. Each person is a complex mix of environmental and biological factors[30].

---

[29] Hamer, Dean H, & Copeland, Peter, *The Science of Desire*, Simon & Schuster, New York, 1994
[30] Wilson, *op. cit.* p 18

Applying this understanding to earlier genetic studies, there may have been evidence of a gay gene, but the sexuality for everyone in the samples may not have been genetic, possibly masking the evidence.

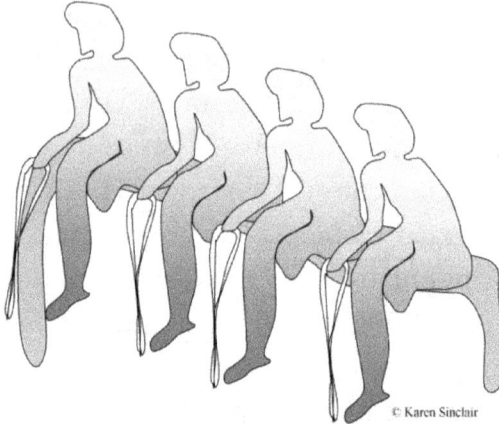

© Karen Sinclair

If a sample population of one legged men was being studied... .... Researchers would need to separate those whose leg condition was natal from those who developed the condition through ... a myriad of other possibilities.

Figure 2: One Legged Research Principle

Other differences, such as hormonal differences between men and women have been over the years defined by scientists. Although these are accurate biological markers, they are not visible to the naked eye or perceptible without

78

scientific equipment. Science has also found ways to administer hormones to influence other recognizable biological differences, as seen in the case of Mark becoming Maggie. These hormones produce effects, including reducing or promoting facial hair growth, breast development and such characteristics that we use to acknowledge the two genders of the human race. Those characteristics affected are perceived in social interaction. That is to say, we are not aware of all the roles of hormones, but our reference point takes us back to the very gender characteristics that triggered the search. In a circular method therefore, our findings are related to our search parameters which are influenced by our cultural reference. We see hair growth as sexual, find the hormones that control it, then we use the evidence of that growth in declaring sexuality and in defining that hormone's role in it.

The jury is still out on biochemical DNA as an indicator of sexuality. Advances in DNA analysis do reveal gender. However, if we regard sexual identity as a dynamic factor that expresses more than gender, it is difficult to conceive of DNA that could predict the varieties of sexual identity and orientation. This is so not only because of the perceived varied assortment of sociosexual behavior patterns, but also because of their variations from culture to culture and from time to time. That is, while DNA may be a constant in human biology, contemporary sexual identity varies temporally and spatially.

Studies of human sexuality, including those referred to previously by Hamer and Copeland, revealed that sexual preferences and orientation can change over time. This view is supported by scientist Barbara Katz Rothman in her book *Genetic Maps and Human Imaginations*[31]. The conclusion is, in a nutshell, that our behavior and conscious action determine our lifestyles, *despite* our genes.

---

[31] Rothman, Barbara Katz, *op.cit.*

CHAPTER 4: THE SOCIAL SENTENCE OF THE SEXES

"We don't make music—it makes us."

David Byrne[vii]

Socioeconomic Perspectives

Historians and anthropologists trace human cooperative efforts back to what they believe to be more than 250,000 years of human history. Work roles in society have historically mirrored gender roles. For society to function today in its historic pattern, roles are identified by our modern culture and to a large extent continue to mirror gender roles. Gender roles take effect for each of us from birth. For the most part, individuals acquiesce with these roles. In discussing socioeconomic perspectives, the discussion centers on work roles– those defined to sustain economic activity.

There may be many reasons for this acquiescence. One such reason may be the thorough process of orienting people from birth to roles defined for them. Another possibility is that since gender roles sustain the society biologically, no roles other than ones that mirror gender can sustain generation after generation.   In other words, the separate work roles prevail because they mirror gender roles, which are biological necessities for human regeneration. We may not know the *reason,* but we do know the result; we are part of a culture that has survived.   One cannot claim that mass acquiescence to gender work roles is a *cause* of human survival; neither can one claim that it is a *precondition* of human survival, but it is clear that like roles of ants in a colony, separation of function continues to prevail in the surviving human culture.

Despite this tacit agreement and acquiescence to gender roles, evidently some people do reject the roles thrust upon them.   There is no knowledge about any identifiable biological trait consistent with rejection of gender roles in society.   Limitations are social, cultural and perhaps psychological.

Another possibility is that role separation may be sustained by human intellect over time. Such an explanation would be consistent with Peter Corning's synergistic proposals that we commit to the traditions we inherit. If Corning is correct, we inherit a habit of acquiescence to separate gender roles and pass it on, strengthening commitment with each successive generation.   In other words, humans get some benefit or satisfaction from it that, over time, sustains each generation's persistence with it.

There are many possible explanations for the relationship between gender and social roles. (I use the term 'social roles' broadly in this context to include 'play' roles, 'work' roles and all differentiated roles supporting activity and organization of the society, including social, economic and other dimensions.) Whatever those reasons may be, it is not easy to separate gender from its social relationships. Studies have documented the behavior of children and tried to filter out the social factor in search of innate reasons for gender roles in our economy. Macoby and Jacklin[viii] concluded that although many studies show some amount of gender differences in the choice of toys in growing children, some form of imitation of observed behavior must be involved[32]. In other words, children imitate what they have previously observed. Their behavior is not based purely on innate triggers.

Further studies by Macoby and Jacklin that reviewed intellectual ability and studied cognitive styles and capabilities such as visual, auditory and touch responses, seem to be inconclusive concerning any consistent observable difference between men and women.

Whatever the details of those studies might be, today we are forced to echo a not-so-new truth that biology does not fully define our capability and by extension, that gender does not inevitably circumscribe our roles. In other words, although our biology at birth sets a particular social path for us, that social path need not be an inescapable life sentence.

---

[32] Macoby, Eleanor E., and Jacklin, Carol N., *The Psychology of Sex Differences*, Stanford University Press, California, 1974, p. 285

The Sentence of Human Survival

One reason used to explain social roles and the different social paths for men and women is human survival. The immortal argument is that because reproduction requires male and female interaction, preserving male female relationships is essential for human survival; and that all alternative behaviors challenge human survival. This is understood. Reproduction requires input from both a man and a woman. Recalling Corning's findings about our cumulative inheritance, one can project the cumulative effect of encouraging different behaviors: over time, occurrence of that reproductive interaction of man and woman would be preserved. Clearly, this cannot be conclusive. Questions challenging this conclusion include the debate about whether permitting challenging behaviors *in addition* to the traditional heterosexual behaviors could indeed eliminate the traditional behaviors. In other words, preserving heterosexuality is not the converse of denying homosexuality or other sexualities, any more than is the preservation of pink roses the converse of denying yellow ones. This argument about preservation of the species will require additional evidence.

Another popular perspective concerns supremacy and power. According to that perspective, one of the ways Man has maintained mastery of the animal kingdom is by upholding reproduction as a fundamental part of his social structure and foundation. In other words, the argument is that one reason that society is based so extensively on sexual roles is that the supremacy of human society depends on heterosexual paring. Without it, mankind would be fewer and fewer and could be reduced to insignificance on the planet. So, according to this perspective, to dominate, human survival becomes wedded to multiplication and hence to heterosexuality.

Survival of the species is an old point of view. In examining heterosexual roles, reproduction is the only function that appears to necessitate the pairing of male and female of the species. Both those points of view are therefore essentially based on the same premise: that heterosexuality is a necessary ingredient in the survival of the species. Let us see what the evidence suggests.

This imperceptible synthesis or blending of social and sexual elements may be termed sociosexual fusion. It is one of the basic universal structures in our modern cultures. There have been other structures. For example, there is on record that the Shakers, a religious sect that bloomed in 1870s New York, denounced sex altogether and also denounced family relationships and marriage[ix]. No member was allowed to have sexual relationships. Ultimately, the cult disintegrated. It is reported that they sought to infiltrate orphanages in order to preserve survival. However, that could not sustain the congregation. Considering its radical policies of celibacy, the cult had no means of survival beyond that generation of its membership. Interestingly, the sect is said to have been started in response to seventeenth century pre-industrial economic suffering and related fatalities as child-bearing women worked[33]. Similar to the extinction of this sect, one can see that unless Man has a certain method to recruit or

---

[33] Stein, Ralph Michael, *A Sect Apart,* Pace Law Faculty Publications, Paper 216, p.6

guarantee new members, as is done through reproduction, humanity's survival could be threatened. Yet, heterosexual culture has survived along with homosexual variations or alternatives.

History has not preserved much information on ancient homosexual cultures. One may presume a similar faith. We hear sketchily about at least one (Sodom), but clearly such cultures have not survived time on their own. In that sense, such a culture may be seen as an appendage to one that supports reproduction. Whatever sophisticated technology, art and culture such a culture may develop, would dissolve and get lost if that society could not survive from generation to generation. This suggests that the reverse of Corning's findings (previously discussed) is also true: that we not only inherit our traditions, but that without some opportunity for inheritance, traditions are lost. Sociosexual fusion weaves sexuality into cultural inheritance, not merely individual inheritances.

In the simplest perspective, a system without the innate ability to sustain its population over time and also to pass on its traditions, can only nurture its own continuity as an appendage to culture that does. If you accept that a society whose fundamental base takes care of its survival is more likely to thrive, then it is easy to see how that society may be more likely to survive both natural and manmade tests of time: survival is fundamental and not the secondary activity it would be if it had been dependent on a separate culture. The logic also applies to the converse. A society that does not nurture the way that it grows and survives over time is not feeding survival.

Part of the reason that a heterosexual society is likely to thrive is that it is able to hand down each little advancement, skill, or idea to a new generation to sustain, develop and improve. Although no sex motivated theories could be found, Joseph Tainter, in his discussion *The Collapse of Complex Societies*,[x] presented several theories to attempt to explain their collapse. Among those is the theory of social dysfunction[34]. According to this theory that he attributes to Jonathan Friedman, some societies no longer exist because their social structures/forms failed. The argument is that "if social forms fail, it is because they have laws of their own whose purpose is other than making optimal use of their techno-environments." In other words, social forms that do not take environment into account are likely to fail.

Although history is littered with failed societies— the Roman Empire, the Byzantine Empire, Ancient Peru—we can only theorize about the precise reason why they no longer exist. There are many theories and it is easy to accept that any or all of them could have happened at some time. We do not know precisely. The theory of social dysfunction is believable. In discussing the fall of the Roman Empire, Tainter quotes Boak and Sinnigen as proposing that the economic system may have discouraged the Roman population to "reproduce in adequate numbers." [35] In the discussion, this indirect reference to reproduction, or more precisely the failure to reproduce, is given as a possible reason for the collapse of societies throughout history. He did recognize the fragility of a civilization as a reason for the

---

[34] Tainter, Joseph, *The Collapse of Complex Societies*, Cambridge University Press, Cambridge, 1988, p. 73
[35] Tainter, Joseph, *ibid.*, p. 69

collapse but did not see it as an immediate threat to today's societies.

Worth mentioning here is that reproduction also enhances the probability of survival from natural calamities and disease. Although large segments of a population may be obliterated in such circumstances, it stands to reason that the ability to reproduce may also secure its re-growth and hence survival.

So, although we do have theories and conclusions, we have little or no historical documentation to explain lost societies. One cannot say that simply because a particular behavior (such as homosexuality) cannot sustain a population biologically generation after generation, then it is any less valid and acceptable within a spectrum of behaviors in society than behaviors that can. Not everyone needs to be a farmer. Continuing the rose bush principle, not every rose reproduces. (An interesting curiosity disclosed by the American Rose Society is that the most sought after highly double roses are worthless for breeding[36].) The ability to sustain itself *may* be a necessary element to guarantee natural survival from generation to generation, but is it a pre-requisite to guarantee survival or to justify obliteration of others' existence at any one time? With that reasoning, it would mean that *at this time* procreation, while it is an element of survival, is not an argument that logically justifies a position concerning alternative forms of sexual behavior. The earlier discussion identified ability to sustain itself as only one of the relevant factors influencing human survival. The ability to hand down traditions was also recognized.

---

[36] Manners, Malcolm M, "A Short Discussion of Flower Structure" www.ars.org

Further, today new babies can be born using eggs and sperm stockpiled in laboratories. If the argument is purely about survival, would stockpiling the elements of reproduction justify homosexual pairing or replace traditional means of multiplying the human race? This is not intended to suggest a solution. The point is, with regard to the discussion of survival, the *capability* exists. Other discussions are still relevant.

At the time of this writing human cloning has been outlawed, but laboratory reproduction and other means of artificial insemination have not been. These are *logical* points and we must recognize that arguments of logic are not the only valid dimension in reason and decision making. The questions of laboratory reproduction and forms of artificial insemination may be considered to be as much about moral and religious *value* as they are about the logic of human survival and preservation. In other words, the promotion of heterosexual behavior may be less about the ability to reproduce, hand down traditions, success in the use of biological techniques and technologies than about moral perspectives and human value, an equally valid dimension.

An alternative society (that is, in this context, a society based on something *other than* heterosexuality) maintains itself as an incidental pursuit. In other words, since reproduction is not fundamental to its establishment, it is also not fundamental to its maintenance. In such societies, maintenance and survival must be separate ventures. In a way then, the cumulative benefit of our ancestral heritage (heterosexuality) is intertwined with our ability to "go forth and multiply". That may be considered to be the basis of the value system of heterosexuality. It is embedded in culture, in everything we do. This means that, while a society can be tolerant of all deviations individuals make from the norm, the fundamental base– the orientation of the masses– takes care of its reproduction and is intimately linked to its survival. There is less likelihood of changing the balance between heterosexual and other groups if there is more education and deeper understanding.

Reproduction is however not the only product of sexual interaction and human sexuality. Wilson[37] identified the sexual bond as of vital importance to human social organization, regardless of any sexual activity. He pointed to additional reasons for the existence of heterosexual social organization, the primary one being genetic diversification. Contrary to the reproduction defense, Wilson's arguments acknowledge that the human sexual urge goes beyond human sexual reproductive capacity and can be felt regardless of ovulation and even during pregnancy. Both these states preclude reproduction. He also suggests that sexual bonding has the potential for reducing aggressive and competitive behavior and accomplishing the social advancements dependent on cooperative behaviors. However, Wilson regards the need for sexual bonding to be independent of the sex (male or female) of the bonding individuals. So, while he makes a strong argument in favor of diversity and cooperation, it does not explain heterosexuality.

The extended array of contemporary sexual identities reflects a more diverse society than that reflected in a purely

---

[37] Wilson, *op. cit.*, ch. 6

heterosexual society. In support of Wilson's arguments about genetic diversification, non-conformity is one of the known marks of creativity and diversity.

There is also the hypothesis based on environmental sustainability. In this hypothesis it is argued that world resources cannot continue to support unchecked population growth. Homosexuality is seen as a natural response to unsustainable population explosion. It would seem that if we examine the concerns of human survival without real world examples, we enter the realm of speculation, surmise, theory and hypothesis. No real world examples could be found to either support or dispute the hypothesis about unchecked population growth, homosexuality and environmental sustainability.

Cultural and legal prescriptions seem to be the only ways to perpetuate 'alternative' lifestyles. Unlike heterosexuality which perpetuates itself and does not require the same cultural and legal maintenance, alternatives do. The hurdle is that legal prescriptions often follow or are inspired by value systems. One contemporary example of the impact of law on reproduction is China where a law was introduced in 1979 to limit some families to only one child each. The law does not apply to the entire population. This stabilized population growth (its goal), while preserving value systems (including heterosexuality). Although that value system was not affected, it may be noted here that the law, as intended, did change the culture evidence in relation to family size. In this light, one can speculate that the celibate Shakers may have attracted new members if the legal and cultural systems had not regarded them as outcasts. The value systems of the time also served to make the cult extinct.

Value systems need not be written or documented. Interestingly, marriage laws in the United States throughout most of its history, did not specifically state that marriage was permitted only between a man and a woman. (This is discussed further in Chapter 6: Law, Policy and Rights.) Yet cultural practices during that time made it so. This suggests that, although laws specifically prescribe behaviors, unconscious value systems are inbred, not necessarily written. It is those systems that kept marriage heterosexual even though the letter of the law was silent. In summary, the discussion of The Sentence of Human Survival reveals that there is evidence that cultures other than heterosexual ones have existed and that in some societies the law has been effective in shaping culture and controlling population growth. One may say that although heterosexual culture may be one factor in human survival, it does not seem to be the only one.

Education, Learning and the Sociosexual Sentence

All social coding is not informal. So far, we have discussed informal forces and influences, as well as inherited traditions and experience-based learning in social coding. We have also looked at what children see of the sexes and how society shapes them by example, persuasion, and negative and positive re-enforcement as they grow into adulthood. Formal and informal education also play significant roles.

Our system of formal education (guided and prescribed instruction and learning) both promotes the culture of straights and sets the foundation for it to thrive. Formal education includes classroom type and other pre-designed official learning curricula, systems and methodologies and institutionalized programs. One is conscious of the formal education experience. However, we do not always understand, nor are aware of our learning, the *informal* education. Ian Stewart and Jack Cohen expressed it pithily in their book "*Figments of Reality*"[xi]. They explained development of the mind as "... the response of an evolving brain to the need to survive in a complex environment."[38] We pick things up with all our senses. We learn to speak simply because others speak to us. Our early language development is entirely based on the languages we are exposed to. If we are exposed to one language, that is what we learn. If our parents speak to us in Chinese, that is how we will speak. Quite effortlessly. We also learn other languages and ways of communicating by what we are exposed to. Expressions of anger and ways to express love, frustration are all learned behaviors. With learning, we need not understand, be instructed, nor be aware.

When we are born we have no concept of "girl" and "boy". These are things we learn. Although it seems that we knew it all our lives, and we may want to think that we were born with this knowledge, someone has to tell us we are a boy or a girl. With that vocabulary also come the social emotions and value judgments. If we had no idea of what these things are, how could we have value judgments about whether they are good for us or whether it is what we want to be?

---

[38] Stewart & Cohen, *op. cit.*, p. ix

There are many who argue that a child may be born not wanting to have a penis, or a teenager not wanting to develop breasts. It is not clear how a child would have an emotion about his or her appendix, toes or sexual organs. How would the child acquire that thought? That is not clear. It is understandable that 'penis envy' could develop in children. However can we conclude that it is a sexual or gender issue? Could the possibility be eliminated that the cause is the visibility and functionality as little boys pee and play garden hose type games that completely exclude little girls? The behavior is one dimension, and the interpretation is another. When a child looks at others, he or she may want to be blond, have red hair or long hair or the penis they admire on someone else. There need not be anything sexual about penis envy in young children. It may be about play and the childish envy of the friend's fancier 'toy'. In other words, it may be similar to the social yearnings prevalent between 'haves' and 'have nots'. It could be a mistake to consider penis envy in young children at play as if it were a gender disorder or even a gender statement. It may also be a mistake to dub a child's refusal to fit into prescribed social roles as a medical ailment or a biological defect. As social beings, not every manifestation of difference is an ailment or medical or biological condition. Further, not every social difference requires treatment. If we can accept that all the white people in a tanning salon are not trying to change their race or even make a racial statement, then could yearning for different body parts not be something other than a sexual statement?

Although primarily a function of our early parenting and home life, what we learn also comes from the entire society we are exposed to. This is consistent with the thinking of Harry Stack Sullivan.[39] Learning here is explored as wisdom that is transferred unconsciously, often without instruction.

Education, on the other hand, is used in this book to refer to a formal process that refines that learning. It may alter, enhance, and expand the learning base. At its best, it will expand our horizons beyond our learning and even break the invisible walls of education and take individuals and the society into new realms of understanding. We don't know exactly where learning begins and education takes over. In fact, the two may dance perfectly in tune with no recognizable ending, or beginning. For example, as we learn language from our family/ social circle, we effortlessly learn grammar and complex construction and vocabulary. However, we also expand our vocabulary, gain insight and understand the rules of grammar and sentence construction through education. In that perfect 'dance' we improve our language skills and at the same time apply rules that enhance the language as a more precise communication tool expressing unambiguously the things we want to communicate.

This is also the way we learn about our sexuality. It starts with the subtleties of example, exposure and observation. But we are not as careful with it as we are with our language. While most of our learned behaviors are acquired through education, most of us go through our entire lives without any education whatever about our sexuality. We are educated about things and about works, but hardly about spheres of influence, thought and perception. There are

---

[39] Sullivan, Harry Stack, *op. cit.* p.70

numerous curricula explaining sex, sexual activity, sexual biology, sexual diseases and birth control. But we are still to see curricula educating us about our sexuality, identity, inclination and orientation; curricula that expand on the rudiments of our learning.

As a result, we have a society that is, at one extreme, almost oblivious of rudiments of its sexuality, and at the other, is technologically sophisticated. Like wild orchids in an open field, it is a society that blossoms and flourishes without fully understanding the human process, particularly our sociosexual make up.

In the 1930s, Gordon Childe, in discussing the revolution in human knowledge in his book "*Man Makes Himself*," explains how the early Egyptians passed on knowledge about astronomy used to guide them in agriculture, and how the Babylonian establishment of a calendar influenced their lunar interests. He also discusses early Oriental art and Sumerian scripts and our inheritances from Arab and Indian mathematics. However, he lamented the absence of evidence of man's understanding of himself, and passing this information on to subsequent generations[40].

This deficiency in education about human sexuality makes many people genuinely believe that sexuality is a static prenatal disposition. To the contrary, in her writings on neurochemistry, neuroscientist Candace Pert[xii] presented the findings of scientific research confirming that there are tiny pieces of protein (peptides) that coordinate "physiology, behavior and emotion toward what seems to be a coherent,

---

[40] Childe, Gordon, *op. cit.*, p.177

meaningful end"[41]. Applying these findings where the coherent meaningful end is sexuality may lead to a different, more dynamic understanding of sexuality over the span of an individual's life.

There is a tacit agreement in our western culture that we not analyze and understand our sexuality. Yet, as explored in Chapter 1, it is the silent master of all our activity. Ignorance about the rudiments of sexual behavior is a norm. Sexuality is considered something of a private choice or a personal privilege. With that silence and exclusion from our formal systems of education, even in our liberal culture today, sexuality remains shrouded in a dirty cloak. As a result, many people are titillated into their sexual learning. We cope with it as a society by introducing sex education at younger ages and more recently to geriatrics in nursing homes, in both cases *pursuing the objective of stemming the tide of disease, and* not pursuing the goal of understanding ourselves. Titillation, not education is at the root of contemporary sexual behavior.

As a society we respond to the evidence of young people's curiosity about sex by controlling their access to sex information, but we do not supplant it by developing an equally robust body of information on sexuality. An examination of education curricula shows hours of work on technologies, while learning about self when not accorded specialty or higher education status, is often extra-curricular. We do not recognize the trail of social influences on our behavior and there are many people who genuinely believe that their sexual behavior is independent of society. As

---

[41] Pert, Candace B., *Molecules of Emotion*, Scribner, New York, 1997, p. 68

Mary Grey puts it in discussing the female experience of sexuality, "the task of hearing the silence into speech is complex, involving the way cultural constructions of gender identities—both masculine and feminine—serve the interests of the powerful; the internalization of both women and men of the dominant understandings of sexual meaning."[42]   In other words, we internalize the external influences of the society and this is reflected in the gender we project.

The Pool of Religious Perspectives and Beliefs

The Encarta English Dictionary defines religion as "people's beliefs and opinions concerning the existence, nature, and worship of a deity or deities and divine involvement in the universe and human life."   These belief systems are often contrasted with science because they do not rely on scientific evidence or proof.   Proof or lack thereof has no effect on people's religious beliefs; neither do beliefs have to be sustained objectively.   With reference to a handful of religions and beliefs, this section will discuss the impact of these perspectives.

When people talk about the spirit it is usually understood to be referring to the religious conception of what that embodies.   However, there is a physical, observable manifestation of the spirit that can stand scientific observation.   This is my observation of the spirit in tangible form: Alzheimer's and dementia are diseases affecting the mind.   It invades intelligent behavior and memory.   As the

---

[42] Grey, Mary, *Embracing Sexuality*, Selling, Joseph A.,(ed.), Ashgate Publishing Co., Hampshire, 2001, p. 61

disease progresses, the individual becomes increasingly incapable of functioning in a way that demonstrates the presence of intellectual thought and action, that is, deliberate action controlled by learning and education. When that intellect is stripped away, we can observe the unclothed spirit of the human being.

I have spent hours in the presence of a dementia patient as she progressed from being a healthy intellect through the decline to what is a severe deficiency in intellectual communication and action. I hesitate to comment on her ability to think intellectually. Thought is only observable through communication and action. No one knows what we think until we express it in some form. So I do not have the ability to assess her ability to think, but only her ability to communicate that thought and to convert it into action. At some stage of the disease, those abilities are dissipated almost completely. However, a strong healthy loving "something" of the person remains present. Doctors Castleman, Gallagher-Thompson and Naythons in their book "*There's Still a Person in There,*"[xiii] presented a similar conclusion[43] in their discussion of Alzheimer's disease. That "something" that I call her spirit is still evident and able to touch you. Nevertheless, the Alzheimer's case presented by Castleman and others profiles the individual in a state without the appearance of cognitive ability. English vocabulary has not developed in the direction that enables us to describe spiritual phenomena apart from the way it manifests itself in the physical dimension such as in communication and action, other than to express that a

---

[43]Castleman, Michael, et. al., *There's Still a Person In there,* G.P. Putnam's Sons, NY, 1999, p. 29

person is still 'in there'. The case of dementia helps us to recognize that the inclinations and tendencies of the spirit transcend the capacities of the physical body. Although medical science neither knows the causes of Alzheimer's and dementia, nor yet fully understands the diseases, clearly reasoned thought as evidenced by communication and action is compromised. That compromised circumstance demonstrates for us that there are fundamental aspects of who we are that are independent of reasoning, judgment and physical presence. In applying this observation to human sexuality it provides a perspective from which to view the potential for influences on individual sexuality more profound than the observable body and the presence or absence of particular sexual organs. Though we lack clear understanding of human development, who is to say that particular sex organs determine who we are sexually? We can hardly conclude with certainty even that they are inextricably connected.

The education and nurturing of the spirit of an individual help to shape deep seated commitment to some specific role in society. As a culture that focuses on tangible, recognizable, observable matter, we have historically ignored the development of our spirit as a necessary part of an advancing civilization. Instead, reading religious texts (The Bible, the Koran, the Torah etc.), which many consider to be the door to the spirit, has, beginning in the late twentieth century, deliberately been removed from western educational curricula. This removal co-incidentally or not, roughly paralleled the end of the industrial revolution and the beginning of the information age. Under the guise of 'separation of Church and state' in the United States, this removal from state funded curricula, has in my view effectively created a vacuum in spiritual understanding in those who depend on the state for their education. As a result, there is a disconnect between education of the mind and rounded development of wholesome people. To that extent, separation of church and state pairs highly educated minds with vacuous or underdeveloped spirits. For evidence of this, one may find cases of brilliant academics with no outward sign of deficiency, committing violent crimes against humanity. In other words, deficiencies of the spirit are not filled by our formal education system. Our systems of reward also no longer champion the causes of spiritual development. There is no vocabulary to discuss it; therefore as far as our culture is concerned the spirit does not exist. Some people today consider spiritual concern irrelevant, receding in importance to a world that is proud of its mastery of the physical environment. In the face of the pressures of physical life, discussion of the spirit looms as an uneducated, immature, archaic digression. The narrow perception of humanity as primarily physical beings is bedrock for confusion in individual human development and particularly with regard to dissonance in individual sexuality which is not merely a matter of physical sexual organs.

One could not complete a discussion of the impact of our society on our sexuality without discussing the influence of religious dogma. It is one of the institutional dimensions of our traditional existence. Religion asserts value systems and controls on human behavior. While federal laws compel people to adhere, people have to decide whether they will adhere to religious prescriptions. When it comes to human sexuality, religious teachings expose individuals to additional dimensions of sexual awareness. In the case of the Catholic Church, it is awareness of procreation. From Philip Sheldrake's discussion in '*the human erotic*[44] in the 2001 publication *Embracing Sexuality*,[xiv] one recognizes that the Catholic Church does not overlook aspects other than procreation. They may be defined a bit differently from today's common description– but the relevant point here is that other functions of sexual activity are acknowledged. In that discourse, Sheldrake differentiates between sexuality and its expression and makes judgment prescriptions about *renouncing* expression, not sexuality: "we may renounce certain forms of sexual expression." In this context, we may consider Janet Smith's discussion of Pope John Paul VI's *Humanae Vitae* prescriptions for the Catholic Church[xv] It is a discussion about contraception that seems equally applicable to discussions of homosexuality:

> *An act of mutual love which impairs the capacity of bringing forth life contradicts both the divine plan which established the nature... of the conjugal bond and also with will of the first Author of human life. For this capacity of bringing forth life was designed by God the Creator of All according to specific laws.*
>
> *Thus, anyone who uses God's gift [of conjugal love] and cancels, if only in part, the significance and the purpose... of this gift, is rebelling against either the male or female nature and against their most intimate relationship, and for this reason, then, he is defying the plan and holy will of God.*[45]

This is one way that religion adds to the pool of 'options' (including limits) an individual may be exposed to. It

---

[44] Sheldrake, Philip, *Embracing Sexuality*, Selling, Joseph A.,(ed.), *op. cit.*, p.32

presents its followers with a perceived role and purpose as intelligence to guide their behavior. It contributes and nurtures values, not merely prescriptions relating to activity.

Different denominations of the Christian Church adopt variations of this approach, with the central ones including principles and standards concerning contraceptives, gay relationships, marriage, monogamy, family, faithfulness and other rules. These rules do not absolutely *determine* their members' choices, but establish values, color the decision-making process, add to the pool of choices of some members and expose others to values relevant to making these choices. The values may have an impact on behavior even when members do not conform. Members may experience guilt or hide the sexual behavior that is inconsistent with the rules and commandments that they are expected to follow. Some simply move on to other groups or become passive members, restricting their participation. Still others, members or non-members, may challenge the rules, form groups and lead protests.

In the Methodist Church, the information in the pool of choices is the Methodist perspective, according to *The Book of Discipline*[xvi], that "Homosexual persons no less than heterosexual persons are individuals of sacred worth. This discipline takes the position that all persons need the ministry and guidance of the Church in their struggles for human fulfillment, as well as spiritual and emotional care in reconciling relationships with God, with others, and with self. Although the Methodist Church again reconfirmed at

---

[45] Smith, Janet E., *Humanae Vitae*, The Catholic University of America Press, Washington, 1991, , p. 102

its general conference in 2012 that it does not condone homosexuality and considers this practice incompatible with Christian teaching, it affirms that God's grace is available to all. It commits to being in ministry for and with all persons."[46] While rejecting particular practices, the Methodist Church in its social creed, repeats this commitment to avoid passing judgment on individuals:

> *The visible Church of Christ as a faithful community of persons affirms the words of all humanity and the value of interrelationship in all of God's creation.*
>
> *In the midst of a sinful world, through the grace of God, we are brought to repentance and faith in Jesus Christ.*[47]

Edward Wilson's discussion about human bonding[48] challenges some of the religious postures with regard to homosexuality. In particular, his finding that human bonding is essential but independent of the sex (male or female) of the bonding individuals, is worth restating here.

Religion also brings hope beyond self and presents an entire system of beliefs, values and expectations completely apart from legal and local considerations. Religious doctrine also adds some meaning to right and wrong. In that sense, religion presents a reason for acting one way or another, and sexual prescriptions are often only one small aspect of some of the religious belief systems. However small, it nevertheless introduces guidance and pre-consideration into what is often regarded as an untamed, natural act of instinct.

---

[46] Olson, Harriet J., (ed.), *The Book of Discipline of The United Methodist Church*, The United Methodist Publishing House, Tennessee, 1996, p.89
[47] ibid, p. 108
[48] Wilson, *op. cit.* p. 6

That is not to suggest that membership in a belief system reflects conformance. There are enough public examples of behavior failings in churches and failures to uphold beliefs to support this view point. Values alone do not determine individual action. It is just one dimension in the pool of influences.

One tenet of the Christian belief system is the triumph of the spirit over the body. Many denominations of the Christian faith seek to strengthen members' abilities to surmount challenges of the physical world. "Lent" for example is a period in the Christian calendar during which some denominations urge their members to give up some form of pleasure, typically some particular food, particular drink or particular social activity they enjoy, for a period of at least forty days. The goal of the Lenten experience is not merely denial of the body, but moreso the strengthening of the ability of the individual spirit to assert its superiority over bodily pleasures. That period of forty days is 'training,' as it were, for Christians to be guided by higher principles. Christians are called to be guided by spiritual principles in the Holy Bible, over, and in preference to, the demands of the body. Similar to other aspects influencing human behavior, the impact of religion is a very individual variable. Options made known through religious contact enter one's pool of choices. The more choices in a pool, the more options an individual can perceive and the more complex is the decision. That is not to say that a particular value system in one's pool of reference makes a person committed to that particular value system. The reality is that one does not have to support a particular point of view, or a particular recommendation, commandment or posture because it is in

105

one's frame of reference. At the same time it is also true that one does not have to belong to or understand doctrine to respond to its influence. In that sense, people do have free will and respond differently to both conscious and unconscious influences.

The pool of prescriptions within a person's frame of reference is not only one of religious values. It includes our instincts, as well as all the influences of society, culture, family, education, religious prescription and public information on scandals, bullying and other events which serve as controls, to name a few influences. Each response is complex, resulting from the interplay of biology, spirit and environment. Whether partly or perfectly within our sphere, whether we agree or not, religion puts options and perspectives of gender, sexual image, sexual identity and orientation in the pool.

Musician David Byrne's keen observation quoted at the beginning of this chapter, is profound insight into the way perspectives assume postures of reality. Similar to the way we perceive music as if it was something created by man, so too do our perspectives of socio economics, survival needs and religion adopt postures of truth in our lives and establish solid belief systems that may be no more real than our thoughts.

A social tradition labels us at birth ... a pronouncement, akin to a judicial sentence, made based on observation of a single biological factor- genitals.

Figure 3: The Sociosexual Life Sentence

CHAPTER 5: THE SENTENCE AS INTELLECTUAL ACTIVITY

Exploring the assertive role of thought and knowledge in sexual activity

Intellectual freedom vs. Biology

The concept of traditional sexual identity being a life sentence was introduced in the first part of this book. That discussion traced the root of the sexual identity by which we are known to a social tradition that labels us at birth, and to the widely shared presumption that genitalia alone are required for identity and for declaring gender for the life of the individual. Sexual identity in that sense is not regarded as biological or genetic. Instead, it is a pronouncement, akin to a judicial sentence, based on observation of a single biological factor– genitals. This discussion focuses on the intellect and its impact on that sentence of sexual identity. The discussion of intellect here refers to the human ability to think and reason. It is contrasted with the emotional feeling or instinctive actions which are considered to be beyond reasoning.   As Mortimer J. Adler asserts in the prologue to his book "*Intellect: Mind Over Matter*"[xvii]:

> The human mind is the same at all times and all places, and... all linguistic and cultural diversities are superficial, the products of differences in nurturing, as compared with the underlying sameness of human nature and the human mind since the origin of the species.[49]

This statement by Adler further expands on the conclusions made earlier about traditions and biology.   When Adler's perspective is applied to human sexuality, we can say that intellect is universal, but differences in development underlie the differences evident in our sexual interests and practices.

Internet Dating—Revealing the Sexual Intellect

Communication over the Internet in Internet chat rooms and dating sites provides the opportunity to virtually separate biological man from intellectual man. As described in the earlier discussion on attraction, in this environment, people get interested in each other independently of real biological interface.   In Internet chat rooms, words represent the individual and are read and interpreted by others. If the writer discloses that he is male, or that he is a teenager, or that she is has long hair, those disclosures are read by the recipient, processed as acceptable or unacceptable and may be worth/ not worth further communication. This will happen whether the disclosures are true or not. In essence, the writer and the recipient are

---

[49] Adler, Mortimer J., *Intellect: Mind Over Matter.*, McMillan Publishing Co., NY, 1990, p. XIV

both stripped of their true biology. Before video and other options were added to the communications options, Internet connections relied entirely on text, and written and read words *became* the total person. No other sense was evident other than the predispositions people brought to the interpretation of the text communications. The communication itself was, in that manner, stripped of sensual exchange except through interpretation of words. Without video, there are no visual stimuli leaking biological information. Before video technology was introduced into Internet dating, use of one or more photographs was an option, although not everyone used a photograph in their dating profile. Clearly, since those Internet communications removed the personal contact that could alert the human senses, if the person could not read, they could not respond sensually through text. This means that the response is entirely determined by intellectual processes, the process of reading, understanding and interpreting. The intellect that is receptive, positively predisposed to the information presented will also be positively disposed to following up with some form of communication in the physical realm. In this sense, it is not the biology that stimulates the interest, but the interest that stimulates the biology.

This perspective suggests that although we may be sentenced by a particular biology, our intellect intervenes in what we do about it. In this case, mind does reign supreme over matter. The evidence that people do bond through Internet connections, including connections with false and misrepresented identities, suggests the presence of sexual intellect in human interaction. Sexual intellect, the use and application of learning and astuteness in sexual behaviors, depicts the assertive role of thought and knowledge in sexual activity. If no intellect had been involved and those bonds depended entirely on physical dimensions, no bonding would occur via the Internet. People would hardly connect to a misrepresentation which had no material, physical dimension or which contradicted the physical reality. Yet, there are reports that people do connect to false representations as in that of a heterosexual woman being unknowingly seduced by a woman who misrepresented herself as a man—a sexual connection that could not have occurred if it depended on biology or some divine instinct. Instead, it suggests that we rationalize and analyze our sexual connections based on information. That evidence does not, however, provide any conclusion about exactly how that sexual intellect is nurtured.

Although the Internet may in this manner be regarded as a virtual laboratory that enables us to separate the influence of physical and biological factors from intellectual and emotional factors, it is not the perfect laboratory. Firstly, the profiles often contain some description of biology. Even without photographs for visual confirmation, this means that whether that information is true or false, its influence on the reader can hardly be determined. Additional research in some controlled study may serve to better determine these influences. Controls may include or exclude photographs, descriptions and reference to certain other factors. At this level, one can only determine that the biology is not the determining factor in the interaction. Another difficulty is the separation of intellect (reasoning) from emotion (feeling) in relationships between the sexes. While differences between the two are not central to a study of the imprint of the social sciences on human identity and orientation, the processes that shape them are, and they both do color the conclusions.

Rejecting the Sentence

So far, the discussion has focused on the original identification at birth of the gender or sex of a child and the predetermined lifelong roles prescribed by society based on that gender. As we saw previously in discussion of cases, such as when Mark became Maggie and when Betty got dressed, that predetermined role or life sentence is not always satisfying to every individual. Rejection of the sentence is not new. There are the "pull" factors that fuel desire to emulate someone else. That emulation may include genetics, hormones, DNA and social science imprints of sexual role modeling that may begin at early ages. Those imprints are the subject of this discussion.

In addition to "pull" factors, "push" factors that may also be part of the social imprint. "Push" factors are concerns or issues that make one gender role seem undesirable or less attractive than another. Their effect, whether conscious or unconscious, is to turn people away from particular roles, behaviors or types of people. Either or both "push" and "pull" factors may influence individuals.

The point is, when we look at individual cases we can hardly know the special circumstantial influences on behavior or their biological predispositions. We do however need to be conscious of the conclusions we arrive at and know that they are only perspectives, and that these conclusions, each time we observe some behavior in a child, will re-enforce our perspective. This is consistent with what Harry Stack Sullivan referred to as "the illusion of personal individuality"[50]. According to this perspective, we grow through and with each other. This would mean that individuality is only an illusion, and that we share responsibilities towards growing children. When in our charge, every response, action and statement of ours reinforces not their perspective, but ours— inherited through our interconnections with them.

Stories have been told of little girls sexually abused by male adults, who in later life have difficulty in personal relationships with men. These provide vivid accounts of how push factors can channel individuals into particular relationships. While events are easy to recognize, more subtle occurrences over time, particularly in the home and social environment, though less clearly defined than an event, can lead to similar dispositions. We also do not understand the role of biology in all this. Therefore, as we review the contrasting paths to rejecting the sentence, perhaps the social barriers to doing so could recede from our shared intellectual horizons. In other words, unless people can appreciate both push and pull pressures, whether heterosexual, homosexual, intersexual, etc., they would hardly perceive the social imprint.

---

[50] Sullivan, Harry Stack, M.D. *The Fusion of Psychiatry and Social Science*, W.W. Norton & Co., New York, 1964, pp. 198.

Enjoying the Sentence

The "sentence" is a biological one. Nurturing and the influence of society shape our appreciation or rejection of that biology. Just as the path of rejecting the sentence is paired with both push and pull pressures, the task of enjoying the sentence is one of finding peace with our lives. In today's society, people take different paths to that destination.

The degree to which one accepts the defined social roles for the gender identity declared at birth appears to have a direct relationship to the degree to which one enjoys the full manifestation of identity. In that sense it appears that it is not so much the declared identity, but prescribed roles and what is expected of a person with the particular identity. For example, a man who prefers to be a woman, may not so much hate being called 'man', but may hate being expected to wear pants and marry women. Similarly, a woman who prefers to be a man may don aggressive postures, wear pants and want to have female sexual partners. Similarly, a man may not reject the pleasure afforded by his male sexual organs, but may be strongly averse to getting that pleasure from relations with women, averse to being limited to doing so, and be unable to do so. In other words, it is the paths, the roles and not the outcomes and effects that are unappealing. It seems that while rejecting the sentence opens a path to one's dream identity, to enjoy the sentence, one embraces the socially defined roles for the assigned identity. A man or woman enjoying the sentence loves themselves, thinks he or she is "the best", loves their sexual organs and takes pleasure in their bodies, and all body parts, however small or big. It is a social role they copy from the icons in their gender and embrace. Sexually they learn how to obtain pleasure from their sexual organs and go about the processes of doing so, meeting people, dating and forming permanent or temporary connections in whatever circumstances they find themselves. The quality of social life is enhanced because not only do they accept themselves, but society also accepts their behaviors.

The truth is, people do not make organ to organ connections, but person to person connections. There are dimensions other than compatibility of the sexual organs that are operative in human sexual connection. Orientation is also not the fundamental magnate since not every heterosexual man is compatible with every heterosexual woman or vice versa. Not every gay man is compatible with every other gay man, or gay woman with every other gay woman. This highlights that people must rise above hurdles other than sexual identity. The opportunity to enjoy one's sexual life, whatever one's orientation, is not limited by gender, identity or orientation. People connections involve a wide spectrum of considerations, including social, aesthetic and others. Learning about one's self and appreciating whoever one is and one's circumstances at any time are key to unlocking life's experiences.

CHAPTER 6: LAW, POLICY AND RIGHTS

Proponents and opponents clash, not on principles of equality, but on different beliefs concerning human sexuality.

American Equal Rights

The United States enacted the Equal Rights amendment to its constitution in 1972, after a long battle of almost fifty years. It took several years to be ratified across the states. The primary motivator at that time was equal opportunities for women in what had been legally a male dominated society. Looking back today, it may seem ridiculous to those born into a climate of equality that the thinking at the time presumed male superiority. But to get the law passed at that time, women had to convince the courts not only that they were being subjected to unfair treatment but that it mattered. At the time, the society accepted the unstated rule that women were the inferior, weaker, insignificant sex. Equal opportunities for women became constitutional but, that amendment did not bring equality opportunities to all groups of people. Homosexuals in the military did not receive equal acceptance. Similar to the unstated presumption about women's inferiority, there was an unstated presumption about homosexuals that allowed the society to simultaneously maintain policies that reflected an unequal perspective about homosexuals in the military. Although the equal rights amendment was passed, a military "Don't ask, don't tell, don't pursue" policy was introduced two decades later and remained in place for almost another two decades.

"Don't Ask Don't Tell" Military Policy

The seed of the "Don't Ask Don't Tell" military policy was first planted in law in the 1950s when President Harry Truman signed The Uniform Code of Military Justice (UCMJ), which included discharge rules for homosexual members[51]. Over time there have been many changes to those policies[52]. The Don't ask, don't tell" policy for example, introduced under the Clinton administration in 1993, changed military policy so that service members who stated that they were homosexual would avoid discharge if they proved that they had no intent of homosexual activity. In that approach the concern surrounded activity, in violation of first amendment rights to free expression. Despite this, discrimination continued.

As recently as March 2007, the Chairman of the Joint Chiefs of Staff, called homosexuality "immoral" and likened it to

---

[51] See "The Uniform Code of Military Justice" www.loc.gov
[52] "A history of 'don't ask, don't tell'", http://www.washingtonpost.com/, Nov 30, 2010

adultery.[53] There was at least one case in which the first amendment was cited, that of National Guard 1st Lt. Andrew Holmes, who lost his position in the Navy after announcing that he was gay.[54] Until it was repealed in 2011, the Don't Ask Don't Tell policy prevented anyone from serving in the military if they *admitted* that they were homosexual. Although the 2011 repeal was a historic change, article 125 of the UCMJ which criminalizes various sexual acts, including homosexual acts, was not simultaneously repealed[xviii], effectively maintaining the status *quo*. This meant that the Equal Rights Amendment of 1972 did not protect homosexuals subject to the military UCMJ policy of the 1950s. The subsequent Don't Ask Don't Tell policy of the 1990s, intended to protect homosexual rights, also fell short. Even that repeal has still not lifted the potential for discrimination under existing military policy. It must be noted that the climate in 2012 appears to be one of tolerance and President Barack Obama expressed his commitment to equal rights. In that climate, article 125, though still on the books, may be a moot policy, but it is left to be seen if policies which remain on the books, such as article 125, will be used against service personnel.

Domestic Partnerships and Civil Unions

Homosexuality was considered a crime throughout the United States until some time in 1962, when the state of

---

[53] Lusero, Lisa, "Military Chief Says Homosexuality is Immoral", www.palmcenter.org, March 13, 2007

[54]Supreme Court of the United States, "Brief for the Federal Respondents In Opposition", 98-500, October 1998, See: http://www.justice.gov/osg/briefs/1998/0responses/98-0500.resp.pdf

Illinois first introduced laws making acts between consenting adults legal. Yet, it was not until more than forty years later, in 2004, that same sex marriages first became legal after the state of Massachusetts became the first to rule that gay couples had the right to marry. By 2012, marriage between adults could be legally performed in seven of America's fifty-two states (Connecticut, District of Columbia, Iowa, Massachusetts, New Hampshire, New York, and Vermont.) However, the situation is not static. An eighth state was scheduled to make it law by 2013, and one state that had successfully legalized same sex marriages in 2008, had that law overturned within six months.

By 2012, a handful of other states enacted legislation governing Domestic Partnerships or Civil Unions. These state laws are not at this time backed by federal legislation. The state of New Jersey for example, passed a law providing for "domestic" partners that assigned benefits and privileges to couples of same sex. The law converting domestic partnerships to civil unions "recognizes the establishment of civil unions between same-sex couples in order to provide these couples with the same benefits, protections and responsibilities that are enjoyed by spouses in a marriage."[55] This law came into effect on February 19, 2007. It creates a new understanding giving recognition to sexual partnering. In that regard, it may be considered to be purely a sexual understanding and sexual recognition since other traditional family partnerships based on similar associations (except for the fact that the individuals are not sexually involved) are not entitled to the same benefits and protections under the law. For example, adult siblings living together can still be

---

[55] N.J.S.A. 37:1-28 et. al. (P.L. 2006, c. 103)

specifically excluded from insurance policies, while sexual partners can be included. Similarly, households including adult children, adult children taking care of elderly parents, or parents taking care of adult children are not recognized for similar benefits by these new laws although they are equally valid and enduring domestic partnerships. By establishing these partnerships simply so that benefits could be awarded, the law may be considered based on principles different from marriage. In contrast, traditional marriage partnerships have in the past been established based on vows, "for richer, for poorer", and often acknowledge and pledge a less material purpose and goal, even though similar benefits do accrue.

In this manner, the law in effect established preferential treatment for particular individuals simply based on their sexual bonding. Without overtly stating this, sexual bonding has become a legal qualifier for distinguishing persons that qualify and those that do not under this law. This category of domestic partners/ civil unions has been granted privileges not awarded others who have equally strong family, love and commitment bonds, but who are not involved in a sexual relationship with each other. The legal definition of "family" has *in effect* been changed, but only to the extent that it recognizes sex as a distinguishing factor of the spousal relationship, while traditional marriage pivots on commitment and contracts of long term devotion. That is the power of the challenges wielded against the heterosexual status quo. In this case it moved from lack of recognition at one extreme to a somewhat privileged status at the other.

In this sense, what appeared firstly as an attempt to recognize homosexual partners, did not only give recognition, nor stop at according equal status when compared with other relationships, but went even further. The new New Jersey Domestic Partnership Law unintentionally accomplishes a sort of supremacy over some of the other forms of domestic alliance in the social pool.

The underlying quest of appeals of the biological sentence is for other forms of association to become socially recognized on equal footing as the heterosexual forms we are sentenced to from birth. In this sense gay couples want to be regarded in the same way as traditional married couples. Significantly, this quest recognizes the social milieu (marriage and family) in which the heterosexual unity derives its importance and validity, while declining the heterosexual culture. This is evidence that the issue is not perceived sexuality, but dissent about being cultural outcasts.

There is nothing biological about marriage, it is a social construct. Some might say a religious construct. Its importance in society is learned, even as our relationships are learned or instinctive. We were not born with a yearning to be married, either heterosexually or homosexually. It is true that bonding of one kind or another may be instinctive, and recognized social units bring order to the cooperative actions of society. But let's face it, we were not born with a yearning to hear someone say "I now pronounce you man and wife". That supports the conclusion that the urge to get married and the pursuit of marriage rights and entitlements under the law, is a social quest somehow embedded in our psychological makeup. People wanting to be married are in fact yearning for a social role, social recognition... reflecting a psychological state.

To get beyond these appearances, questions about the role of social acceptance in validating our sexual paths need to be explored.

Social Acceptance and Marriage

As discussed, domestic partnership and civil union laws permit persons of the same sex the financial benefits of traditional (heterosexual) marriage, despite incomparable levels in the status of the benefits of social acceptance. It means that the distinction between the two can no longer be quantified since no benefit is forfeited, denied or differently awarded. Removing that ammunition is a win for the culture of straights. Although it is progress for those attacking discrimination against gays, it does nothing for the level of social acceptance of gay relationships.

Theories of belonging and group behavior uphold social acceptance as a human psychological need. Whatever the laws are, domestic partners and civil couples still face a separate challenge to the social concept of marriage. However, law may indeed be the easier hurdle. As acknowledged earlier in this book, marriage survived as a heterosexual construct in the western world for centuries without any statement that it was strictly for a man and a woman. No one noticed. Men and women got married and that's just the way it was. Harry Stack Sullivan[xix] recognizes this mediate understanding as the kind of experience that is handed down through generations but is equally valid to understanding our direct individual experience. Using that perspective, one can envision that, despite inherited understanding, a new awareness set in (reminiscent of the awareness of nakedness that brought man and woman together in the first instance), and the norm is challenged. Suddenly states have to defend the collective understanding of the law and each arrives at its own conclusion. Each state decides not only whether just men and women should be joined in marriage, but also whether it is legal to deny others the same "privilege". What we learn from this is, that whatever social constructs we establish, we do so with certain assumptions that at the time we may not even be aware we are making. (Like the debated historical assumption that marriage was intended between men and women only). The other lesson learned in these appeals is the truth that whatever social structure we establish will become an operating reality for future generations, although the assumptions and intent may remain silent over the years. Only its perpetuation will serve as living truth. In other words, the reasons for what we do today may be lost with time, but the way we change society lasts forever. Although the reasons for today's domestic partnership and civil union laws may be lost over time, domestic partners and civil couples may very well continue to reap the financial benefits and entitlements of traditional marriage without the complications of marriage certificates, commitment vows and the divorce process that burden heterosexual couples, but also without the full benefits of social acceptance. Acceptance is based on value assessments and is not the same as written law.

Sexual Identity and Marriage

Traditional marriages require licenses, witnesses and are performed only by individuals vested by law with the power to do so. In addition, society frowns on marriages made for purposes of acquiring citizenship and other material benefit. "Gold diggers" are condemned. Civil unions and domestic partnership requirements are in contrast with this. In reality, any two people who would like to share insurance and other benefits may register as domestic partners or form civil unions. In addition to opening an opportunity for non-heterosexual couples, it appears to be a way for any two people to declare a family unit for purposes of domestic benefit without the social and legal complications, vows and commitments of traditional marriage. At the time of this writing, self-identification is all that is required.

There is yet no clear understanding or consensus about human sexual identity on which to base legal prescriptions aimed at sexually identified groups. Vague dogma that was accepted as appropriate during centuries of conformity is no longer adequate in the complex, interconnected mass society. As an example, legal and social systems, including those governing marriage and family, have historically been developed on the presumption of heterosexuality and the acknowledgment of two sexes, man and woman. Given the contemporary spectrum that includes intersex, transex and transgender individuals, whose identities may (or may not) be those of man or woman, can these legal and social systems regulate marriage based on sexual identity? The more recent history of change in America includes the 1996 Defense of Marriage Act that defined marriage as an act between a man and a woman. If based on sexual identity, some same sex relationships already proclaim one man and one woman. One wonders if they could not qualify under existing law. Interestingly, the focus is often not on sexual identity, but on orientation. In today's complex world, neither the law nor society has defined whether domestic partners are based on sex, sexuality, sexual behavior, sexual orientation, sexual identity, sexual preference or domestic preference, and neither has acknowledged that each of these may carry completely different implications. Indeed, domestic partners may themselves also define each of these entities differently.

Attempts to change marriage law have over the years encountered many hurdles, not the least of which is the absence of consensus or understanding about human sexuality. Proponents and opponents clash, not on principles of equality, but on different beliefs concerning human sexuality. Sidestepping that issue, a bill in the US Congress in 2012, the Respect for Marriage Act, proposed federal recognition of all marriages between two consenting adults. This proposed change would not encounter hurdles of consensus concerning identification of man and woman and definitions of human sexuality, since it only requires the consent of adults. As discussed in the previous sections of this chapter, marriage is as much a cultural practice as it is a legal provision. Legal man and a legal woman are culturally defined. Marriage law faces the hurdle of the social perception interwoven by history in the culture. It is also interesting to note that similar legislation proposed in Australia in 2012 was not successful. Even if the bill is passed in the United States, it will remain to be seen whether the legal change would herald social change.

CHAPTER 7: SOCIAL CONVENTION AND PRACTICES

"You are a child of the universe, No less than the trees and the stars. You have a right to be here and whether or not it is clear to you, no doubt the universe is unfolding as it should..."

Desiderata

Conformity and non-conformity

The scenario so far is that we learn, are taught and educated, and societies reinforce and highlight various aspects of our existence. But we do have a choice. Individuals have free will, but develop and nurture common behaviors that characterize them as a group. It is not that these groups create member clones who believe and perceive in exactly the same way. Social evidence does not show that to be true. On the contrary, in any of these groups, there are conformers and promoters of the group rules. The study of group dynamics allows us to recognize degrees of conformity and the role of outcasts of each group. Group dynamics define those who are for one reason or another peripheral, on the outskirts of the group, or who challenge the rules and beliefs and choose not to conform. Challenges may stretch group rules and force a group to redefine itself to include particular anomalies; or to reaffirm itself, rejecting the anomalies. In discussing group psychology, Eric Hoffer[xx] presented a similar view of the dynamics of group behavior, uniformity and change:

> *...imitation is an essential unifying agent. The development of a close-knit group is inconceivable without a diffusion of uniformity. The one-mindedness... prized by every mass movement [is] achieved as much by imitation as by obedience.*[56]

Again, group dynamics do not explain the whole story. However, it does define the various pools of influence on the human psyche. Churches, towns, countries etc, create the body of knowledge and understanding that people are exposed to, sip from, learn and join in a constantly growing gestalt-like dynamic process. This argument echoes the Gestalt psychology theory that the whole is greater than the sum of its parts.

What this means for sexuality is that, although people may be confined to gender groups and prescribed roles, each individual brings their qualities to the categories and roles. With this sharing, neither the gender categories nor the identity and orientation could be expected to be static over time.

---

[56] Hoffer, Eric, *The True Believer*, Harper & Row Publishers Inc., New York, 1951, p.99

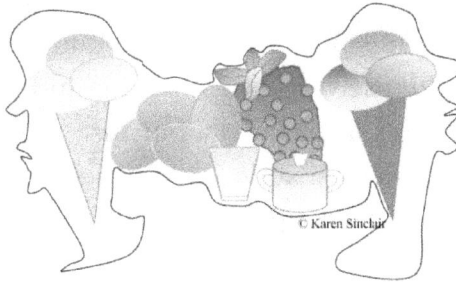

Just as ice cream ingredients (milk, sugar, a few eggs) by themselves have separate and distinct tastes and uninspiring roles in our diets, but fuse together in some mysterious way to make exotic ice creams, so too do these pools of influence in group lives shape and mould and churn and boil to produce individual psyches. Like ice creams flavored with different fruits and nuts and could be crunchy, creamy or savory, human life experiences and exposures flavor our preferences and create diverse nuances in each of our lives.

Figure 4: The Ice Cream Principle

The Ice Cream Principle

Peter Corning labeled this process 'synergy' and discussed it as Nature's Magic[57]. In layman's' terms, I like to call it the Ice Cream Principle. Just as ice cream ingredients (milk, sugar, eggs) by themselves have separate and distinct tastes and uninspiring roles in our diets, but fuse together in some mysterious way to make exotic ice creams, so too do these pools of influence in groups shape and mould and churn and boil to produce individual psyches. Like ice creams flavored with different fruits and nuts and could be crunchy, creamy or savory, human life experiences and exposures flavor our preferences and create diverse nuances in each of our lives.

The pools of influence also define the constraints that are set up for people, and label members based on these characteristics. In that circular manner, membership offers specific options within which members develop, practice and explore their innate compulsions and influence the options. In other words, people teach and are taught the rules of the group. It is a process that Dr. Stack Sullivan considers as the fusion of psychiatry and social science[58]. We each process that information and it may or may not sit comfortably with what we already know. It is easy to conform if there is no discord between what we are taught and what we already know or believe. The tough part and the frustration arise when the two do not accord. Learning is so subtle, however, that as is often the case with discord, people do not necessarily have a clear picture of the exact reason for

[57] Corning, Peter, *op. cit.*, p. 277
[58] Sullivan, Harry Stack, *op. cit.*

discomfort. In this way, social conventions and practices become inextricably melted into the individual, while at the same time, the original distinct 'flavors' of each practice are absorbed by the whole, like ice cream ingredients, not to be overcome or consumed, but to become part of the unique character of an individual person. The Ice Cream Principle does not judge and evaluate individual distinct parts such as, biological gender, sexual identity, insecurities, education, etc., but regards the whole person without judgment as a valid manifestation of humanity. Although the Ice Cream Principle acknowledges individual dimensions it does not separate specific qualities from the whole person. Basing acceptance on sexual orientation separates sexuality from the whole person, like tasting eggs and milk with sugar instead of enjoying ice cream.

That feature of the Ice Cream Principle helps to highlight one of the hurdles to acceptance. The process of "coming out" was referred to earlier in the book as an occasion when a person declares his sexual identity. In doing so, the person draws attention to one specific aspect of his identity, the sexual aspect. Like pointing out to someone who feels that eggs are not good for you that it is one of the ingredients in the ice cream he is enjoying, coming out highlights for traditional society one ingredient that colors acceptance. While coming out may provide inner satisfaction for the person making the assertion, it speaks loudly about sex, which heterosexual society generally keeps private. The silent master, defined in the analysis in Chapter 1, makes an unexpected public appearance in a coming out event. That it is a non-heterosexual appearance is only part of the issue. The other part, perhaps even the greater affront to tradition, is the public divulgence of private information about one's sex life. Coming out gets attention, exposing not merely a gender, identity or orientation difference, but making a sociocultural misstep by the sex talk when no other group is talking. It is understood that the culture of straights does not *need* to hold public conversations about their sex lives. This discussion merely points to the potholes on the path to acceptance.

Extelligence

This term was coined by Stewart and Cohen to refer to the knowledge and the impact of our collective cultural material, ideas and concepts. Our brain, it seems, is stimulated by the cultural environment, such that there are nuances of difference for each of us depending on the specific sounds, information and other stimuli detected by it. Understanding extelligence helps us to recognize and acknowledge our brain as a dynamic system with an interactive relationship with our environment. Our abilities and consciousness both shape and are shaped by it. Our intelligence is the understanding of that information, while extelligence is the body of information accessed or perceived by the individual. This body of information is so important to the individual that Dr. Harry Stack Sullivan in his book *The Fusion of Psychiatry and Social Science,* previously cited, even questioned the fundamental concept of "individual". He argued that given the overwhelming influence of the environment in determining and shaping personality and behavior, each personality is "an indeterminate entity some significant characteristics of which may be inferred from the processes that occur in the group of persons—real and fantastic— in which the [person] participates."[59] According to this perspective we are indeed not "individual" but largely a 'feature' of a larger organism.

In the discussion of The Shape of Identity in Chapter 1, reference was made to the crucial psychological importance of social interaction on the human psyche as confirmed by the rapid psychological deterioration of prisoners in solitary confinement. Whether or not we fully understand the process by which it occurs, the collapse of the psyche in those circumstances is testimony to the sustenance the psyche obtains from association with other humans. Hostage syndrome similarly reflects how intrinsic human values can be changed by the situation. The discussion of extelligence furthers these perspectives. Whether it is because of dependency, human survival instinct or the simple fact that the captor *becomes* the available society, it is not easy to determine. Other possibilities, such as the passion and dominance of the captor's cause and the strength of captors' commitment to their cause, can only be speculated upon as possible evidence of the syndrome. But this uncertainty about the *reason* does not deny the *existence* of the syndrome and the importance of extelligence in development of individual identity– how the person sees themselves, and on orientation– how the person relates to others.

The importance of the syndrome in this discussion is the demonstration of the deep psychological dependence on others within proximity. We thrive on others. Clearly, who

---

[59] Sullivan, Harry Stack, *op. cit.*, p. 70.

we are and what we value are shaped and molded by the values and pursuits of our society and how we understand them. This perception extends the horizons of extelligence defined by Stewart and Cohen as far as the horizon of the *perceived* society that nurtures those values.

Clearly, the insight we gain about captivity and subjugation does not alone explain human behavior. For example, the enslavement of Africans by international traders that began some time in the fifteenth century, persisted as a viable social and economic system for some three hundred years. However, the slaves ultimately fought their way out of slavery despite environmental pressure and the fact that generations of subjugation had created a cocoon for the development of mass hostage syndrome among them. Firstly, slavery was a worldwide system. All the superpowers of the time supported the system— the British, French, Spanish, Portuguese, American– everyone was plundering Africa and Africans. Having been uprooted from their own shores, the perceived society of enslaved Africans became the society of white dominance. Yet, they did not succumb to the system and become docile participants in their own enslavement. Why? Is it some superior intellect, stronger mental acuity? We do not have that information. We do know that the social horizons in their perception were consistent with this image of white dominance and white superiority and perpetuated it. Yet slaves continued to fight the system.

It is not the purpose of this book to present a full analysis of slavery and how it persisted for some three generations. The relevant point here is the pervasiveness of the social system in dominating the *actions* of even unwilling participants without necessarily changing the *will* of the participants and their desire for something else. Applying this analysis to the understanding of the human psyche, one may say that although circumstances may determine human *actions* they do not necessarily change or create human desires, yearnings and hopes. Particular behaviors may be response to particular circumstances and need not define the nature of a person. The fact that the abolition of slavery itself resulted in these same people seeking to take an equal place in the society, speaks to the interplay of intelligence with extelligence.

Extelligence refines the understanding in Chapter 1, clarifying that it is not merely the operative facts in the environment but the *perception* or *understanding* of those facts that comes to bear on the individual psyche. When applied to identity, we see how the way people define themselves is not wholly an intrinsic conception but influenced by extrinsic perception. By extension we may refine understanding of the role of environment in the array of sexual identities as the body of environmental facts from which individual sexual identity evolves: the scope of individual extelligence, subject to individual intelligence.

Applying the extelligence perspective further suggests that traditional sexual identity is the root of contemporary sexual identities, each being a fragment, extension from or evolution of traditional, and is not a separate, alien phenomena. The history of sexual identities may therefore be a procedural outcome of the dynamic created by extelligence, beginning with the original two sexual identities, male and female. In other words, man is neither a static biology nor is he a delimited and inhibited intelligence, but a progressive growing biological, intelligent and extelligent being. From two sexes with a single heterosexual relationship with each other, contemporary society is witness to growth of a network of relationships through extelligence. With regard to what this may mean for human sexuality, we may conclude that changes in the environment may not result in changes in intrinsic desire but behavioral changes; and changes in the *way* people perceive and satisfy their desires. Yet it need not be predestined or unstoppable. Indications are that hostages and prisoners of war generally go through some form of "debriefing" to relieve burdens of captivity. History shows that slaves did this without the debriefing offered to hostages and prisoners of war returning to society. Either way, this suggests that who we are as individuals is not shaped merely by circumstances.

In brief, this analysis points to the limits or perimeters of our understanding and perception of determinants on human behavior. It acknowledges the role of extelligence that limits, defines and prescribes our actions and the scope of our behavior. It suggests that sexual *behavior,* can be a circumstantial response to environment, but does not circumscribe the non-behavioral dimensions of our sexuality. Particular sexual alliances may satisfy emotional (or other) needs but cannot be taken as definitions of the only ways those needs may be met. Instead they may very well be definitions of our time and place.

In essence, the discussion validates the human sexual drive without linking it irreversibly with any person or thing external to it. Simply put, we are sexual beings. Period. The details of our behavior and perception are environmental perceptions. Consistent with this, the Hamer and Copeland studies[60] demonstrate that self-identity varies with different circumstances at various times in peoples' lives. The conclusion is that it is more a discernment than a fixed constraint.

The concept of extelligence also has implications for understanding social movements. In the late 1960s, the then Governor Ronald Reagan of California refused to back down from declaring homosexuality to be a "tragic disease" that should be considered illegal[61]. That was the climate at the time. Power can carry greater weight than appeals to logic, reasoning, fairness and even legal arguments. Nevertheless, Ronald Reagan, as President in the 1980s, was seen by the Independent Gay Forum as not having acted on that declaration[62]. In the same light, stripped of emotion, the fight for new social systems, viewed in the context of extelligence, is little more than power play based on our perceptions of situational information, in this case, the new morality compared with the old.

In summary, the concept of extelligence defined by Stewart and Cohen updates the understanding so far of sexual identity and orientation. Sexual identity is not merely given at birth, but develops (involuntarily), grows (through nurturing), and blooms (intelligently) in the context of extelligence. Fully bloomed, sexual identity displays biological, innate, intelligent and extelligent components. Sexual identity sprouts orientation as a live attribute of man

---

[60] Hamer & Copeland, op.cit., p. 63
[61] Thompson, Mark, *op. cit.*, p.5
[62] Carpenter, Dale, "Reagan and Gays: A Reassessment", Independent Gay Forum, June 10, 2004

from biology and spirit, shaped and pruned by nurturing, watered by intelligence and dynamic extelligence.

Behavioral Freedom- The New Morality

The presence of groups displaying various and conflicting forms of behavior suggests that today's society accommodates diverse behaviors. Different support groups exist for example to encourage anorexia and to discourage it. Different groups also exist for those in favor of abortion and those who do not support it. With the prevalence of these groups, each new generation gets the message that freedom with respect to everything is a right. There is no singular society. There is no one value to be upheld. The modern society is plural, diverse, and permissive of virtually any behavior that does not trample someone else's freedom.

In that regard the society appears to have no shared morality or even shared courtesies and expectations. In a general sense, today we can no longer depend on shared social or cultural beliefs or perspectives of reasonableness. There is no consensus of right and wrong, courteous or indiscrete. A clear demonstration of this in the United States is the way rules governing the use of modern technology are handled. Rule makers have turned to law to establish limits even on courtesies such as cell phone use[63]. To that point, one city in America even established a ban in 2012 on large sizes of sodas to encourage particular eating behaviors. The ban included the sale of sweetened

---

[63]Cell Phone and Texting Laws, www.iihs.org, September 2012

beverages in containers larger than 16 ounces.[64] By repeatedly taking this route to shape behaviors, society today is progressively one in which the pivot of behavior is not what is right or wrong or for the common good, but law and the fear of punishment. It is within this climate that the new morality thrives.

The pursuit of happiness is by no means new. However it appears that modern American man looks to egalitarian laws to set limits. Social behaviors are heirs to both the thread and the loopholes of the legal fabric. That is to say that there is no social consideration of right or wrong other than legal guilt or innocence according to the precise letter of the law. In this sense, one may say that written Law encapsulates the social value system and people accept as fair and unblemished any behavior that is not specifically excluded from law. The social context is one in which progress and change are inextricably linked with interpretation and formulation of written law. Although sexual behavior is a private affair, it is not immune to the influence of this context. Significantly, the quest for new definitions of marriage has taken a legal path.

To further understand the context of sexual behavior in modern society, one must also understand modern morality. We may get a perspective of today's morality by looking at lawsuits pursued by ordinary folk. In a recent case, individuals filed a lawsuit against a fast food chain for serving them fast food. The chain later reviewed its menu offerings, whether as a result of this lawsuit or not, I don't

---

[64] Grynbaum, Michael M., "Health Panel Approves Restriction on Sale of Large Sugary Drinks", www.nytimes.com, September 13, 2012

know. In another lawsuit, a man sued his dry cleaner for millions of dollars for a pair of pants worth close to one hundred dollars. This is the behavioral context of American morality. The judgment for standards of behavior is what the law allows.

In a simple society it is easy to maintain consensus. In a huge complex community of people from different backgrounds, experiences and values, concepts of right and wrong become complex and multifaceted. Without a shared morality or consistently shared beliefs, tacit concord and ethics give way to more formal rules, which, unlike shared beliefs, may need to be justified and explained to people holding different convictions. This is consistent with the separation of belief and law (Church and state). In practice and deed, America is not governed by "In God we Trust." Formerly, that shared mantra needed only to have been placed on the nation's coins. Today, belief has no unanimity, religious trust is optional, religious beliefs are individual choices, but law is inclusive of all morality. In this context, there is no universal morality to adhere to except the precise letter of the law. In that sense, the new morality *is* the precise letter of the law. Values, ethics and principles not precisely stated in law are challenged using law, and there is no standard to challenge behaviors and occurrences not specifically outlawed. Instead, each new challenge encountered is met with new legislation.

Therapy

There are some who have proposed therapy to shape individuals whose orientation and/ or preferences and/or identity may be different from heterosexual expectations. The Christine Bakke story broadcast in a 2007 television program[65] described the therapy as one that focuses on, in my assessment, behavioral change, verbal conformance and the social fashions of sexual identity such as accessorizing. This is not surprising, given the understanding gleaned from the previous discussion concerning acceptance of behaviors and fashions as an indication of identity, including sexual identity. To a large extent there is tacit acceptance that those behaviors and fashions illustrate human sexuality. Whether people identify as "gay" or "straight", there is a common shared social standard about what those words mean and what sexuality is. Not surprisingly, Christine Bakke, who on the television program described herself as gay, explained that the therapies did not work. From the foregoing analysis I propose the view that the need is not for therapy. Instead, the need is for education and learning, building a body of knowledge to influence likes, dislikes, principles, values, character and will. There is a flood of influences, known and unknown, on human choices, behaviors and dispositions. People may be educated to recognize what they are and better understand themselves and each other. Therapy without understanding could prove futile. Establishing goals of therapy based on social indicators of identity, without understanding the human psyche may be misguided. Religious definitions are also used to justify one kind of sexual behaviors or invalidate another.   Yet, religious justification is not adequate. Although they establish goals and value systems, religions fall short on understanding the human psyche and conveying that understanding in a manner that reaches people today needing help on the journey.   Most benefit would accrue if the source is non-partisan.

To illustrate the value of understanding, I will share a little anecdote about the role it plays in influencing behavior. Some years ago in the early days of my computer career in the telecommunication industry, I operated a punched card machine.   One of my jobs was to merge the telephone billing records into a particular sequence for monthly billing. I was about 18 at the time, fresh out of high school and fascinated by the machines.   I asked my supervisor, a competent, no-nonsense expert in the job, whom we will call "Tony", why the process was done that way.   Tony told me very simply and clearly that that's the way it was done. So, the next time I was left alone to do the merge, I decided to do it a different way. And it worked... Right up to the last step. I was excited! Then the process failed during the last step. Only then did I understand why it was done the way it was done. Perhaps Tony just didn't think that I deserved an explanation, perhaps he couldn't explain. Whatever it was, that is not the issue. The real issue is the creative urge to push boundaries and enter new frontiers. Sometimes the issue is not one of ability or inability but one of will. New frontiers breached in industry and technology are testimony to human curiosity. Human beings have the capacity to act in many ways and similar to learning to drive a car, fly an airplane, or operate a computer, they can obtain satisfaction

---

[65] "Woman Speaks Out About Gay 'Cure'", ABC News, April 23, 2007

by following particular rules. Any therapy to enforce particular rules or behaviors may need to satisfactorily explain why.

Jacquelynne Parson's collection[xxi] of studies of the psychoneuroendocrinology of sexual orientation may be of value in providing explanations. Those studies provide insights into the mind and biology behind observed sexual differences. The involvement of both body and mind suggests that therapy that needs consensual participation requires a known, shared standard or value. The participant must buy-in not only to the expected outcome, but also to the underlying value of the therapy. My view is that a successful therapy whether it is for an eating disorder, a broken heart, a sexual habit or some destructive behavior, addresses not only 'how' but 'why'. Granted, it is easier to address the expected change, than it is to address the reasons governing a particular behavior. But both mind and body must be addressed. It is also easier if specific social, physical or other consequences could be defined, but not so easy when the consequences pertain to a belief or value. Values are internalized, behavior is more obvious. Putting someone on a diet presumes a shared value about eating habits that the diet is expected to correct, perhaps a shared value about health or aesthetics. Yet, there are other dimensions. The cause of the habit is another. Recommending a diet without understanding why someone eats the way they do, is futile. Similarly, sexual therapy that pivots on religious value presumes that the individual shares the value and implies a particular cause. Religion is only one sphere of influence. Without the 'preacher' first understanding tenets of that person's attraction, desire, preference and orientation, shared value only establishes a beginning, perhaps a goal. An attempt to change behavior without that understanding is based on presumptions. Cookie-cutter therapies were consistent with the historical assumptions of the culture of straights. Today's complex society demands greater understanding of the individual.

Studies of connections between the human psyche and the human body in sexuality confirm the connection between mind and body. In the Parson studies of the psychoneuroendocrinology of sexual orientation previously cited, Meyer-Bahlburg explained that hormonal treatment aimed at changing male homosexuality was unsuccessful in changing sexual orientation, activity, potency or libido.[66] This has implications for the analysis and understanding of orientation. Today the treatments are used mainly to promote an individual's consciously chosen sexual direction.

To conclude, this analysis suggests that goal oriented therapy without clear values is presumptuous, cosmetic therapy. It presumes a standard of what is normal, or right, or wrong or healthy or unhealthy, and superficially addresses the evidence, ignoring cause and source. Even with shared values, for example religious values, therapy without understanding is ineffectual. Today's therapies may incorporate examination of a spectrum of influences on individual sexuality. Therapy to force particular sexuality is an imposition of the historical culture of straights and needs to be re-examined.

---

[66] Parsons, Jacquelynne, *The Psychobiology of Sex Differences and Sex Roles*, Hemisphere Publishing Corp., 1980, p. 112

Surgery

The term 'cosmetic surgery' is often used to refer to elective surgeries, but I will attempt to avoid it here since inferences about whether sexual surgery is fundamental or cosmetic may prejudice the objective discussion. Whether surgery is considered elective or imperative often depends on who recommends or requests it. Surgery recommended by a medical professional may be considered imperative based on a medical diagnosis. However, a doctor may help a patient identify suitable options, discuss and make suggestions based on a patient's desire. In this discussion, if a patient opts for surgery for a condition for which there is no medical diagnosis or need, it will be referred to as elective.

Elective surgeries are often sought to change bodily appearance. Those relevant here include surgery either to enhance or diminish existing sexual features as well as surgical changes to look like someone of a different sex. In either case, the changes affect visual identity, how a person looks or is perceived. There may be a variety of motivators including age, functionality, aesthetics and sexuality prompting elective surgeries. This discussion will focus primarily on the motivation as it relates to sexuality. The discussion will not consider relationships that may or may not exist among the motivators.

The sexuality motivation seems to have at least two dimensions: what an individual feels inside, and the perspective that people are not seeing the individual the way they want to be seen. Whether influenced by the feeling inside or the view from outside, each individual develops a physical image of the person they would like to be. The image of that person may come from some intrinsic kernel or be conjured from the people they have encountered through socialization. These people may be real, fictional, religious, historic, imagined, or other individual or combination of people however encountered. The influence may serve to favor qualities in others that individuals want to emulate, to prejudice individual preferences against others, or to clarify new paths for those who want to be unique. Another compelling influence is the knowledge of what one's society expects.

Wherever the urge comes from, the step toward elective gender surgery is an assertive one to change the physical body. There are those who see the body as an obstacle to the expression of their sexuality and pursue elective surgery to cross that hurdle/ align the physical body with their sexual perceptions. It is not that the body is insensitive to pleasure, neither is it dysfunctional. In cases of gender reassignment surgery, the goal is to surgically reconstruct existing genitals to form those of the opposite sex. The surgery disposes of unwanted portions but reuses the same tissue to form the new organs. In these surgeries, a penis is swapped for a vagina and scrotum and testes discarded. Alternatively, ovaries and vagina are swapped for penile prosthesis. Of course the surgeries are not that simple and often involve major interventions such as hysterectomies and breast tissue construction. The result of the surgeries is superficially correct anatomies with no guarantee of functionality[67]. Commitment to sex change may involve life threatening risk. Yet, surgeries do not resolve social and emotional issues. National Society and Culture columnist Tammy Reed reported in her article on gender reassignment surgery that a patient who was socially or emotionally unstable before the operation was likely to remain socially or emotionally unstable.

Today, there is a surge in elective surgeries. This surge is both a function of modern technological development (it is more sophisticated and invasive than widely available in the past), and contemporary economic well being (if you can afford it). But the urge to change the body is not new, neither is the urge to assume a different identity. In discussing transvestites (cross dressers), Helen Boyd[xxii] who is married to a cross dresser, pointed out that cross dressers tend to go unacknowledged. She concluded that this is primarily because they are heterosexual.[68] However, whether we recognize them or not, cross dressing is not a new phenomenon. People may often presume homosexuality when confronted with cross-dressing. However, Helen Boyd's story confirms the difference between fashion and sexuality. Her husband identifies himself as heterosexual, although he lives his life dressed as a woman. Because surgery is mostly irreversible, it may be important for anyone embarking on gender assignment surgery to distinguish between the expected physical transformation and the social transformation that wearing different kinds of clothing accomplishes. Dressing and cross dressing may be viewed as superficial encounters with social maleness or

---

[67] Reed, Tammy, "Gender Reassignment Surgery", www.examiner.com, December 3, 2011
[68] Boyd, Helen, *op. cit.*, p. 11

social femaleness. The clothing, whoever wears it, projects a particular gender image. This perspective points to the role of human socialization. Cross-dressing does to the gender image what elective surgery does to the physical body. Both adjust features of individual identity. Considering the invasiveness and level of risk involved in surgery, including risk of life, permanent scarring, loss of sexual functionality, as well as the uncertainty of success, suggests that the individual sees its goal as fundamental to existence. It characterizes gender assignment as a primary issue of life and death for those individuals.

From the information provided, the surgeries do not merely align the physical body with existing hormonal or genetic sexual make up. Instead, as revealed in the discussion of Margaret Stumpp's transformation[69], these surgeries may also be accompanied by hormone and other therapies to establish and maintain the new sexual identity. The effect then is not one of changing the outside to match what is already inside; it is more of a complete internal and external remake and transformation. This could explain Tammy Reed's conclusion that socially or emotionally unstable patients remained socially or emotionally unstable following surgery. In other words, the surgeries transform manifestations of gender, not fix social or emotional instability.

---

[69] Geller, Adam, "Margaret Stumpp - Changing gender, keeping a job: Can a company cope when Mark becomes Margaret?" Associated Press Archive May 19, 2003

Perspectives of Orientation

Earlier in the book we discussed how male and female gender identities are assigned at birth and that other sexual identities are asserted or assumed later in life through social and medical means. Sexual orientation is related to sexual identity and relationships between particular sexual identities. Orientation is defined as positioning, inclination or leaning. When we discuss sexual orientation we are, as it were, looking at where people are positioned sexually in relation to others. It can be viewed as a sexual relationship 'yardstick". This yardstick is a complex self-determined measure that is often derived from likes, dislikes, desires, feelings, activities, behavior, habits and social expectations, emotions and preferences. That is generally what orientation is. While identity is more about self, (i.e. the person and who that person is), orientation considers how that self relates with others.

In discussing orientation, we need to separate what orientation is from how we recognize it. Sexual orientation may manifest itself in behavior. For that reason, social behavior needs to be distinguished from sexual behavior. Behaviors may be considered social if they maintain and promote the collective wellbeing of a group of people. Sexual behavior on the other hand is the interaction of people for purposes of accomplishing individual sexual satisfaction. Social and sexual behaviors are often aligned but they are not the same. Individuals may also have goals beyond collective wellbeing when they socialize. These include individual goals, antisocial goals, and destructive goals. Even more complex is the myriad of individual goals, which may include sexual goals.   This discussion will distinguish between social and sexual association as the association of people for purposes of societal wellbeing, on the one hand, and purposes of accomplishing sexual satisfaction, on the other.

Many cultures encourage socializing in groups of the same sex. Our culture is rife with groups and associations, teams and clubs that separate men and women for various social purposes. Women also get together over coffee, lunch and go out to occasions together, and so do men. This may be considered social behavior. People who often and repeatedly socialize this way identify themselves as heterosexual. They are exclusively interested in partnering for sexual purposes only with people of the opposite sex. In those cases, these behaviors have nothing whatever to do with sex or sexual desire.   In that sense, these are homosocial behaviors.   Individuals sometimes find the company of the same sex a refuge and respite from the stresses and demands of heterosexual relationships. They may themselves be partners in a satisfying heterosexual relationship and may also find this form of socializing to be a way to sharpen their feminine or masculine identities. In that sense, homo*social* behaviors may be an important classroom as it were, or forum to build and reinforce solid heterosexual identities that are markedly different. Pursuits and activities may be different and so may be the informal structures and behaviors of the separately socializing sexes. Homosocial behavior may therefore be the cocoon for a successful heterosexual society.   It is important to distinguish between homo*social* behavior and homo*sexual* behavior because, although some social interaction may be inspired by sexual pursuits, not all social behaviors have anything whatever to do with sexual orientation.

Contemporary definitions of sexual orientation include words such as 'preference' and 'interest'. Preference suggests choice, while interest implies conscious behavior, both of which seem prejudicial to a neutral discussion. The term sexual orientation will be used here without prejudice, to refer to an individual's predilection or inclination toward specific types of partners for sexual relations.

One consistent truth about sexual orientation is that it is often a matter of self-declaration. No proof is required, there is no standard to meet, no vow to uphold, neither does the basis of an individual's assertion about sexual orientation have to be consistent with that of another person's assertion. Self-identification is the accepted vehicle for conveying sexual orientation. There are exceptions, such as situations where parents draw conclusions about the sexual orientation of a minor, often based on observed behavior. Pitfalls of this were discussed in the section Social Environment and Identity. Conclusions are subjective and there needs to be no consensus of opinion nor agreement among observers about the meaning of the observed behavior. In addition, traditional, historical and contemporary perspectives about sex, gender, identity and orientation are not the same. This will be addressed in the section on Gender, Identity and Orientation Gio Indexes.

Although this is what the terms mean, these classifications are made based on self-identification and not on any particular criteria. Hamer and Copeland accept the use of self-identification as the most accurate approach to defining sexuality, given the stigma of homosexuality[70]. Even though various behavior traits may be observed in individuals, it is not currently acceptable for anyone to announce conclusions about someone else's sexual orientation.

Another perspective about sexual orientation is that it is about behavior, or what people do. This is evident in the attitudes and prescriptions of some of the major churches. For example, by prescribing behavior appropriate for Catholics, Pope John Paul VI's *Humanae Vitae* discussed in the section The Pool of Religious Perspectives and Beliefs, implies that sexuality is about behavior, and hence that homosexuality and heterosexuality may be prescribed for in the writings of the church. This means that if they hold unapprised perspectives about sexual orientation, some religious, political and other groups that do not *intend* to be unfair or to discriminate, may hold positions that are unknowingly incompatible with their underlying [71]moral principles. However, in reality, sexual orientation may remain unexpressed until the person "comes out".

It is particularly important to understand the foregoing discussion about homosocial behaviors and to distinguish between social behaviors and sexual behaviors in order to clearly understand sexual identity and sexual orientation. Because of the many cultural trappings that define gender for a social audience, including clothing and hair, preferences surrounding these trappings can mistakenly be used as signals of sexual identity and sexual orientation.

---

[70] Hamer & Copeland, *op. cit.* p. 89

Similarly, homosocial activities with no sexual intent may be misinterpreted as indications of homosexuality.

From these various perspectives it is clear that sexual orientation is not something we can assert with objectivity. We may look at it in relation to what we understand or observe about human nature. For example, we may apply Peter Corning's analysis in his book "Nature's Magic"[xxiii] to the understanding of sexual orientation. Corning perceived life as "a multileveled model- from genes to ecosystems and, indeed, the entire biosphere- a model in which the survival units at each level are functionally interdependent "wholes". In this perspective, orientation may be understood as having layers of being and layers of expression. This is consistent with the understanding that a person is a combination of innate, developed and learned qualities in an ongoing intelligent process that is not static over time and in all situations. Passive and expressed components may vary according to interplay of the kaleidoscope of social, genetic and other conditions. To paraphrase the poet John Donne's poem, "no gene is an island."[72]

---

[72] Corning, *op. cit.* p. 315, from "No Man is an Island" by John Donne

Gender, Identity and Orientation (gio) Indexes

*For there are eunuchs who have been so from birth, and
there are eunuchs who have been made eunuchs by men,
and there are eunuchs who have made themselves eunuchs
for the sake of the kingdom of heaven. Let the one who is
able to receive this, receive it.*

Matthew 19:12[73]

The foregoing discussions concerning relationships between
gender, identity and orientation may be summarized in
original, historical and contemporary gender identity and
orientation (gio) indexes. These indexes do not present
new genders, identities, orientations, or new sexuality.
Instead, they provide new lenses through which
contemporary sexuality may be understood. It is logical
analysis that takes into account the empirical and other data
referred to in this book. Although specific examples of each
of the gio relationships shown in the indexes have not been
referenced in discussions, they are all consistent with
implications of the data. In the tables below, as is the case
throughout this book, the terms 'male' and 'man' are
equivalent, as are the terms 'female' and 'woman'.

Original Gio Index

Original gender, considered to be man and woman,
construed two sexual identities and one sexual orientation.
This can be viewed according to the gio index defined in the
table below. In all the gio tables, the first row is the heading
of each column, for example in the table below, Gender,
Identity and Orientation are the three columns of the table.
This means that this gio index has three dimensions, gender,

---

[73] *Holy Bible*, Revised Standard Version, Matthew 19:12

identity and orientation. Each row represents one relationship between columns. For example, in the first row of the table below, man, male, heterosexual is one relationship in the gio index. In other words, the gender man with an identity male and orientation heterosexual represents one gio relationship in the original gio index. This is a simple gio index table with two rows, each defining a single gio relationship. A gio relationship is a way in which gender, identity and orientation are fused in an individual. Looking at the table below, we can therefore say that this original gio index defines two gio relationships.

Gender	Identity	Orientation
Man--->	male--->	heterosexual
Woman--->	female--->	heterosexual

Table 1: Original Gio Index

Historical Gio Index

History recognized the original gender dichotomy but also documented the existence of eunuchs with no sex organs either from birth, through social practices imposed on individuals or from self mutilation. Also acknowledged in history is the presence of people born with both sex organs, hermaphrodites and of homosexuality. Various traditions attempted to identify hermaphrodites as either one of the two gender identities recognized. This is taken into account here, and it is presumed that eunuchs were asexual, although there may well have had other sexual orientations. These factors define the more complex historical gio index. It still recognizes gender-based sexual identity and has three dimensions, but defines seven gio relationships as follows:

Gender	Identity	Orientation
Man--->	male--->	heterosexual
Man--->	male--->	homosexual
Woman--->	female--->	heterosexual
Woman--->	female--->	homosexual
Hermaphrodite--->	male--->	heterosexual
Hermaphrodite--->	female--->	heterosexual
Eunuch--->	eunuch--->	asexual

Table 2: Historical Gio Index

Common terms of orientation- based sexual identity include homosexual, gay, lesbian, same gender loving, SGL, bisexual, transsexual. Related terms of sexual orientation include homosexual male, gay man, SGL male, homosexual female, gay woman, SGL female, transsexual male transsexual female, bisexual male, bisexual female etc... Less common terms include ambisexual (same as bisexual), pansexual, (relationships with all sexual identities) omnisexual (includes pansexual, and persons who extend sexual activity to non-human beings and objects).

Contemporary Gio Index

The Contemporary gio index recognizes an inclusive spectrum of genders, identities and orientations. The index takes into account not only birth factors, but medical and surgical practices, social and cultural influences and contemporary freedom of adults to associate. The term 'straight' is more often used for 'heterosexual', 'gay' for 'homosexual' and 'intersex' for hermaphrodite. Not much information could be found concerning contemporary eunuchs, but they may well be subsumed in the culture of straights. This three dimensional contemporary gio index is more complex than the indexes in the previous two tables. It defines at least nineteen gio relationships. Contemporary gio relationships with more than three dimensions are presented in subsequent tables.

Gender	Identity	Orientation
Man --->	male--->	straight
Man--->	male--->	gay
Man--->	male--->	bisexual
Man--->	female--->	straight
Man--->	female--->	gay
Man--->	female--->	bisexual
Woman--->	female--->	gay
Woman--->	female--->	bisexual
Woman--->	male--->	straight
Woman--->	male--->	gay
Woman--->	male--->	bisexual
Intersex--->	male--->	straight
Intersex--->	male--->	gay
Intersex--->	male--->	bisexual
Intersex--->	female--->	straight
Intersex--->	female--->	gay
Intersex--->	female--->	bisexual
Intersex--->	intersex--->	intersex or SGL
Intersex--->	intersex--->	pansexual

Table 3: Contemporary Gio Index

Contemporary gio is even more diverse than shown in this table. Different individuals prefer different terminology. In particular, the gay experience is sometimes called Same Gender Loving (SGL), the term lesbian is sometimes used to refer to gay women and bisexuals, pansexuals and intersexuals sometimes use the term gay.

Contemporary Transgender Gio Index

Transgender sexuality may be viewed in two ways, either as blending in or as asserting a separate transgender status. Table 3: Contemporary Gio Index may be used to understand blending in, according to the gender someone asserts. For example, according to gender as male, identity as female, and orientation as either straight, gay or bisexual as they prefer. Alternatively, the following table outlines the Contemporary Transgender Gio Index, showing transgender identities. It uses four dimensions and is even more complex that the previous tables. Taking the original sex into account, it shows twenty-six gio relationships.

Sex	Gender	Identity	Orientation
Male --->	woman--->	female--->	straight
Male--->	woman--->	female--->	gay
Male--->	woman--->	female--->	bisexual
Male--->	woman--->	female--->	SGL
Male--->	woman--->	transgender--->	straight
Male--->	woman--->	transgender--->	gay
Male--->	woman--->	transgender--->	bisexual
Male--->	woman--->	transgender--->	SGL
Female--->	man--->	male--->	straight
Female--->	man--->	male--->	gay
Female--->	man--->	male--->	bisexual
Female--->	man--->	male--->	SGL
Female--->	man--->	transgender--->	straight
Female--->	man--->	transgender--->	gay
Female--->	man--->	transgender--->	bisexual
Female--->	man--->	transgender--->	SGL
Intersex--->	woman--->	female--->	straight
Intersex--->	woman--->	female--->	gay
Intersex--->	woman--->	female--->	bisexual
Intersex--->	woman--->	female--->	SGL
Intersex--->	woman--->	female--->	pansexual
Intersex--->	man--->	male--->	straight
Intersex--->	man--->	male--->	gay
Intersex--->	man--->	male--->	bisexual
Intersex--->	man--->	male--->	SGL
Intersex--->	man--->	male--->	pansexual

Table 4: Contemporary Transgender Gio Index

Note that in the transgender gio index, SGL refers to other transgender individuals with similar profiles.

Contemporary Transex Gio Index

While 'transgender' identifies a change in sociosexual attributes to experience a particular gender and identity lifestyle, the term transex identifies individuals who pursue hormonal, surgical and psychological therapies to change their original sex. Like transgender, transex may also be understood in two ways. One understanding is through Table 3: Contemporary Gio Index, above, according to the gender they assert: for example, according to gender as male, identity as male and orientation as straight. Alternatively, the following Table 5: Contemporary Transex Gio Index, helps to understand transex showing transsexual status. It uses five dimensions and defines twenty-two gio relationships.

Sex	Transex	Gender	Identity	Orientation
Male--->	female--->	woman--->	female--->	straight
Male--->	female--->	woman--->	female--->	gay
Male--->	female--->	woman--->	female--->	bisexual
Male--->	female--->	woman--->	female--->	SGL
Male--->	female--->	woman--->	transex--->	transexual
Female--->	male--->	man--->	male--->	straight
Female--->	male--->	man--->	male--->	gay
Female--->	male--->	man--->	male--->	bisexual
Female--->	male--->	man--->	male--->	SGL
Female--->	male--->	man--->	transex--->	transexual
Intersex--->	female--->	woman--->	female--->	straight
Intersex--->	female--->	woman--->	female--->	gay
Intersex--->	female--->	woman--->	female--->	bisexual
Intersex--->	female--->	woman--->	female--->	SGL
Intersex--->	female--->	woman--->	female--->	pansexual
Intersex--->	female--->	woman--->	transex--->	transexual
Intersex--->	male--->	man--->	male--->	straight
Intersex--->	male--->	man--->	male--->	gay
Intersex--->	male--->	man--->	male--->	bisexual
Intersex--->	male--->	man--->	male--->	SGL
Intersex--->	male--->	man--->	male--->	pansexual
Intersex--->	male--->	man--->	transex--->	transexual

Table 5: Contemporary Transex Gio Index

Contemporary Orientation- Based Gio Index

In the gio indexes above, the term 'gay' is used only as an orientation. However, if we can think outside the blinders created by our culture of straights, we can allow that there is more to human sexuality than meets the eye. There is debate that there may be another sex. Even to casual observation, some people *look* unlike male or female, although one is hard pressed to explain exactly what defines them, just as one is hard pressed to say exactly how one can visually distinguish an Italian from a Latin American or German, a Nigerian from an Ethiopian, or an American Indian from an East Indian, yet we acknowledge their existence. One could also be wrong. Gay sexuality may also, like transgender sexuality, be understood in two ways. Those who want to blend in may be understood in the contemporary gio indexes above, according to whichever gender they assert: for example, according to gender as male, identity as male and orientation as gay. The following table accords recognition to 'gay' asserted either as gender or as identity. It also recognizes bisexuality, intersex and transgender in the gio index as if they were themselves gender conditions. In that sense, they advance the discussion into questions about whether they are conditions of male and female identity and gender or separate manifestations of gender arising from factors other than genitals. Eight gio relationships are shown in the table below.

Gender	Orientation	Identity
Gay<---	gay	--->male
Gay<---	gay	--->female
Man<---	gay	--->gay male
Woman<---	gay	--->gay female
Gay<---	gay	--->gay
Bisexual<---	bisexual	--->bisexual
Intersex<---	intersex	--->intersex
Transgender<---	transgender	--->transgender

Table 6: Contemporary Orientation Based Gio Index.

Contemporary Transvestite Gio Index

Transvestite behavior (cross-dressing) is not considered a sexual identity or orientation. The cross-dresser is typically an individual who likes to wear clothing socially reserved for the opposite sex. However, in the discussion of sexual identity and orientation, developing the transvestite gio index may help shed light and clarifications that may be of value to general understanding. Since transvestites may enjoy two states of dress and need not permanently cross dress, the gio index contains five dimensions. Empirical data used in this book, in particular the Betty Boyd studies, imply only two gio relationships, both heterosexual. Logical analysis however suggests that there may be additional gio relationships, such as bisexual, as shown in the contemporary gio index below. However, if other relationships emerge along with the transvestite behaviors, this understanding may suggest that those relationships hinge on more than the vestments or dress. That is where other gio indexes such as the transgender gio index may be more appropriate.

Gender	Identity	Dress	Cross-dress	Orientation
Man--->	male--->	male--->	female--->	straight
Man--->	male--->	male--->	female--->	bisexual
Woman--->	female--->	female--->	male--->	straight
Woman--->	female--->	female--->	male--->	bisexual

Table 7: Contemporary Transvestite Gio Index

CHAPTER 8: BEYOND SEXUAL HORIZONS

"...genes don't fall in love, people do"

Revisiting Human perception

Earlier in the book we looked at how our world is shaped by 'figments of reality' and the limitations of our horizons. The collective human understanding seems to be an incremental organism with conceptual horizons that individuals or entire generations fight against, constantly pushing to see beyond barriers to perception and understanding, buckling the blind barriers of yet undiscovered truths and theories. That collective understanding may be seen as gradually gaining new ground and hitting old barriers with enhanced pieces of information and new technology. It may be seen as continuously creating different theories, none of which is yet the whole truth.

In the earlier discussions, we also profiled birth and recognized various perspectives of the social processes in our lives. Sullivan calls this collective imprint our mediate experience[74]. Similarly, we understand aspects of ourselves and of our experiences, (such as sight, solitary confinement, speech development, sexual pleasure, speed, light, gravity, night, day, and music) by reference to each other's experiences. We collect data and develop knowledge about these things and over time share a larger and larger pool of information and inherited knowledge and theories. Each generation learns a bit more, clarifies a bit more. However, we still never quite answer all the questions, nor have a complete and total understanding of these things. So it is with our perception of our sexual identity and orientation and the imprint society exerts on them.

Distinguishing Learning from Biology

Previous discussions, particularly in the section Education, Learning and the Sociosexual Sentence, included examples showing that in Western society our perception of ourselves is proscribed by western exposure, observation and education. More difficult to appreciate is the truth that our understanding of tangible, physical biology may also be proscribed by our minds. Although we may believe that biology is not influenced by perception, there is evidence that even aspects of our physical biology and its performance may be influenced by belief and the power of our minds.

In this vein, I refer to Harvard Professor Herbert Benson's exploration of the capabilities of the maximized human mind potential in his book *Your Maximum Mind*[xxiv].

---

[74] Sullivan, Harry Stack, *op. cit.*

Professor Benson presents the findings of his 1985 research with Tibetan monks who were able to control their body temperatures in sub zero climate temperatures. This enabled them to spend all night outdoors without even a shiver, even surviving a light snowfall wearing only sandals, loincloth and cotton wraps[75]. Mind control was used there in a technique that the western world does not even attempt.

My contention here is that aspects of what we are and our capabilities may be determined or constrained by something other than our biology. As shown by the monks, this is so even for the endurance and capacity of our biology. I am by no means suggesting that because trained Tibetan monks can determine how their bodies respond to external stimuli, that this is the case for all human biological responses to stimuli. Instead, the monks are presented here as an example illustrating the *capacity* of the human mind and its *potential* influence on biology. This illustration suggests that one can hardly generalize about the social imprint on human sexuality. Sexuality includes identity, orientation, biology and habits of sexual behavior. There is no one entity, but a complex, dynamo with societal and other imprints.

---

[75] Benson, Herbert, & Proctor, William, *Your Maximum Mind*, Random House of Canada, Inc., Toronto, 1987 pp. 15-22

Habit and Lifestyle

Whatever is one's perspective of learning and biology, they both are the raw material of, or inputs to sexuality. Habit and lifestyle on the other hand represent sexuality in action. They are not easy to characterize. Part of the reason for this is that, although we are often open to debate the different bodies of information on many habits of the human condition, it is not so with sexuality. On all sides of the debate it could become a very sensitive issue to relate sexual identity with habits and behavior. There are those who claim genetic pre-dispositions, but although acceptable, this is yet to be documented. There are many belief systems that will not entertain even the possibility of early learning, exposure and habit as a normal part of acquiring sexual identity and developing orientation whether gay or straight. Some belief systems are convinced that being gay is a style of living while being straight is genetic. In this regard, gay traits are seen as socially conditioned and *resulting from* actions, lifestyle and behavior. Others are sure that being gay or straight is a genetic characteristic and would not allow that there are social influences. An objective perspective would examine the processes of learning, acquiring habits and developing lifestyles.

In the earlier discussions of learning in this book, both formal and informal processes of acquiring human behavior were examined. Repeated over time, behaviors become habits. Instinctive behavior would similarly reveal itself over time as habit. Learning and acquiring habits is so subtle a process that we may have no idea of the origins of our traits, character and behaviors. This means that under examination, learned habits are often indistinguishable from habits inspired by genetics or biology. By extension, in the assessment of lifestyles using observation, it is equally difficult to distinguish between learned or acquired sexual habits and behaviors inspired by innate genetic predispositions.

Nevertheless, some of the cases presented in "*The Long Road to Freedom*[xxv], which recounted the history of the gay and lesbian movement, shed some light on dissociative sexual behaviors that could support a more objective understanding. Editor Mark Thompson uncovered the promiscuous world of "tearoom sex" in the context of the movement of the 1970s. In that account, married or single men regardless of whether they had a family, wife or children, presented themselves in restroom stalls of various places throughout the country for furtive, instant, impersonal sexual encounters with men.[76] Those encounters distinguish between lifestyles based on innate, physical hunger for sex and that inspired by some quality in the other person, whether gender or some other factor unrelated to the physical hunger for sex. Although the encounters were reported to be primarily with persons of the same gender, the biological sex of that individual appears not to have been overtly relevant to the acts. Sexual organs were fondled and pleasure served without reference to the persons. The context was *homo*sexual in that the individuals were of the same sex, but the impersonal lack of emotion or personal connection was clinical and dissociative. In these instances, the overt homosexual behavior may also be convenient for heterosexual and other men. They sought

---

[76] Thompson, Mark, *op. cit.* p. 43

a particular kind of sexual act and it hardly mattered who administered the service and what defined the gender, identity or sexual orientation of that person.

Other accounts of the history of the gay and lesbian movement in that book also presented more instances of what seemed to be promiscuity and consecutive sex partnerships in the same sex context that were devoid of gender interest. In other words, it was the service of sex that mattered, not the sexuality, not the orientation, not affection, not the identity, not even—(or so it seems) physical attraction. Repeated descriptions of people in the mode of total abandon and indulgence were presented. This includes discussions such as "Manhattan Hunting Grounds" (p.236) and Safe Sex Parties (p.269) that related sex acts as conveniences for impersonal gratification without commitment, bonding, inhibitions or rules associated with both homosexual and heterosexual partnerships. Sex parties did not require partners. Bodies exchanged pleasure without personal intimacy. These undisguised habits of gratification and excess are used to explain the gay lifestyle of that time. It was a time of unbridled sexual freedom and abandon and appeared to have included both male and female homosexual, bisexual and heterosexual individuals tumbling in tangled abandon. Thompson correctly characterized that time as a moment in the long road to freedom. Although it does not reflect the rationale often presented today, this history confirms that for humans, habits of sex need not be a reflection of sexual orientation.

Public observation of sexual lifestyle today suggests that the public images of the homosexual community include more stable unions and display greater similarities to traditional heterosexual unions. With greater similarities to traditional structures, these couplings are less alien to the traditional perspectives and therefore may be more likely to integrate into the society than the earlier images of the gay community. It could also be a boon on the legal front. By reducing the glaring concerns of promiscuity, related legal opinions could therefore be argued, debated and voted on with a lighter burden of difference from the norm.

Today, gay life that earned its name in the abandon of the sixties and seventies is no longer being painted as any more joyous than heterosexual life. One also sees evidence of greater assimilation into main stream society. For example, today, the term "movement" is not used as often, as the gay community seeks to integrate and show its sameness with the traditional community, establishing stable families complete with children, parents and extended relatives. Further, the term "alternative" lifestyle also seems to have lost its popularity. That word subtly accorded heterosexuality primacy and branded gay life with the stigma of lower esteem, unconventional, or the antithesis of a "preferred" class. Its slipping into disuse may reflect gay integration into mainstream life. Purposes have also shifted: where the early movement sought to end employment discrimination, over time that militancy has succeeded in gradually turning old open discrimination and open hatred into attitudes of public tolerance and official recognition combined with denouncements of expressions and acts of hatred. The trajectory in recognizing lifestyles is evident in current indications of progress toward acceptance through changes in laws and social values.

Nowhere are the subtle lines between learning and biology more carefully tread than in the discussion of sexual behavior. There appears to be unwillingness to accept with dignity that society can influence or determine lifestyle. It is felt somehow that biology is a more acceptable and dignified explanation than is society. Social perspectives today are such that if human behavior, sexual or otherwise, is determined by biology, it gains social dignity.

In connecting early socialization with sexual biology, Dean Hamer and Peter Copeland published a book in 1994 based on research using men[xxvi]. The book included in its analysis social factors such as childhood playmate preferences, sports, as well as the men's personal classification of themselves and a variety of other factors to define particular classifications, gay or homosexual and non-homosexual.[77] I call these sociosexual classifications because they include socially determined factors and perspectives in classifying sexuality. The analysis then pursued genetic analyses related to these (sociosexual) groups. It provides a useful stepping stone toward greater understanding.

One may ponder if further study along these lines may benefit from the perspective that homosexuality may very well have two (or even more) equally valid bases- one of them sociosexual. As one reads the interviews in the Hamer Copeland studies, one must recall that the sample is based on self-identification and standards for doing so are unclear. In that sense, even if there may be a gene, it would not show consistently unless all sexuality resulted from genetics. Recognizing the imprint of society, consideration may also

---

[77] Hamer, & Copeland, *op. cit.* pp. 234-243

be given to the perspective that the sample may have included individuals whose orientation may have been genetically inspired together with those whose orientation may have been socially inspired.

The statistical probabilities used to understand and express findings as these studies do suggest that genetic predictability is not entirely conclusive. This may reflect a need to understand more. It may also indicate room for neutral research goals. Some research efforts seek to justify/ explain sexual orientation with biological features and characteristics. This may be appreciated when it is considered that acceptance of gay rights may be promoted by research findings that show a biological cause. The culture is such that a social explanation may not be considered to be as dignified as a biological. Who can determine whether a person is *being* gay or *doing* gay? Similarly, who can determine whether a person *is* straight or *does* straight? The culture is more tolerant about people *being* gay, but not equally so about *doing* gay. Whether heterosexual, homosexual, bisexual or other, the difference between *being* and *doing* is the difference between hapless recipients of sexuality, and complicit architects of it.

Barbara Katz Rothman whose book *Genetic Maps and Human Imaginations* was cited in the first part of this book, explains this best in the introduction in her book. Referring to genes and DNA as similar to culinary recipes or musical notes she raises the issues of whether genes are causal factors in the people we are. Barbara Katz Rothman argues that despite genes, we can each become completely different individuals:

> *If DNA is a Bible, it's capable of being read in a lot of*
> *different ways... Is it possible that this static thing, these*
> *notes on the page, this string of ATCGs [DNA] is life? Or*
> *is life the process itself in which these and other–notes are*
> *played?*[78]

That is an important question to resolve if law makers are to
use human genetics as a social life sentence. As Rothman
explains:

> *'Shy' genes don't blush; gay genes don't go off to gay bars;*
> *smart genes don't do math. [Genes] have no meaning*
> *without a context: the context is the person and the*
> *intersecting communities in which that person lives.*[79]

In other words, genes don't fall in love, people do.
Rothman's statement that genes have no meaning without a
context is consistent with the perspective developed in this
book that society attaches meaning to our biology. We
collectively develop various social classifications and
lifestyles, and our habits and lifestyles in turn become
wedded to our biology. Her assertion that the context is the
combination of the individual and his/ her relationship with
the community is the perfect spring board for a discussion
of man and his environment.

Man and his environment

To understand why a social explanation plays foster child to
the family of biological research in our perception, we need
to understand modern man's interplay with the
environment. Today, man has conquered distance and
geography, and explored the oceans, outer space and the

---

[78] Rothman, Barbara Katz, *op. cit.*, p. 25
[79] Rothman, *ibid.* p. 222

skies. It is true that man stands out as a species that grows food, converts soils and ores into equipment and devices, converts air into power and discovered and harnessed virtual existence for all to see. Wow! We congratulate ourselves.

As Peter Corning, in his brilliant analysis of synergy concluded in the book *Nature's Magic* about the epic of human life:

> *Now we are gaining control of the ongoing epic itself.*
> *Witting or not, we control the Sorcerer's magic.* [80]

We are so impressed with our accomplishments that we generally believe that we have conquered our environment. However, there is at least one remaining dimension to conquer. Almost the last remaining frontier of our understanding and conquest is man himself. We are constantly working on halting aging, slowing death, conquering birth, understanding debilitating disease. We perform transfusions, organ transplants, nips and tucks and triumphantly boost failing organs with mechanical and electronic devices. Collectively, we accept that we have not conquered biology. We continue to pursue it because we see civilization as the ultimate conquest of every phenomenon in existence. We don't need to explain why. That is what civilization is— constant attack on each frontier. We understand tacitly and we proceed to conquer everything in the environment. Everything that is, except ourselves.

Understanding ourselves seems not to be a general pursuit in our society. When we see that the compulsory first year courses at almost every institution of learning places value on mathematics, economics and technology, it raises no

---

[80] Corning, *op. cit.* p. 318

alarm. We establish space missions, technology research and development, and understand their importance to civilization. So, our kids begin to understand mathematics, never themselves. Understanding ourselves is not awarded equal primacy as a foundation in our education. Instead, there is tacit agreement that what we need to be successful in our world is math, technology and language skill. In those areas we have established universal standards and principles of right and wrong.

There are many examples in the structure and functioning of society that reflect the perspective that there is no 'right' and 'wrong' when it comes to human behavior as long as it does not hinder the life or freedom of another person or group. It appears that in the way he lives and works, man harnesses and tames the environment to advance civilization, but progress for him means freedom of the wild, unbridled *self*. That is the context of the contemporary analysis of sexual identity and orientation.

Conquest of the mind

Despite our advanced intellect, humanity can hardly explain itself. Human life is the last frontier. This shows itself in the sexual aspect of the challenge and the age old heterosexual assumption, particularly the historical dichotomous (male/female) perception.

Whether we accept aspects of ourselves as gifts, or perceive ourselves to be victims or casualties of it, the shared perception is that we are *born that way*. As a people, gay or straight, there are conceptual hurdles to accepting that we do not know everything about how our minds and bodies work. Recalling Herbert Benson's Tibetan Monk experiments and his concept of the 'Maximum Mind',[81] we can perceive that at least for some people, the hurdles are surmountable. Instead, one contemporary approach to an observed dissonance between mind and body seeks the maximum body to be happy in the mind. In other words, the body is changed to meet perceptions of the mind. A person is more likely to be described as trapped by the body than to be described as being trapped by the mind. But, where is the trap? Is a *person* trapped by his or her body, or does *the body* become victim of a trap created by a person's mind? This perception influences the approach to resolving dissonance between body and mind.

Conquest of the mind is a major undertaking. It embraces less tangible concepts than our bodies do. Among these is the symbiotic relationship between the individual and society. In that sense we are all part of a bigger social system; a society that has over time found various ways to cultivate us for *its* purpose. We are not only part of the society but also share responsibility for its architecture. In a symbiotic relationship, both parties benefit. The individual benefits in that society also shapes and gives identity. The truth is: one has no identity without others, without society. Take for example an orange in a bowl of fruit. If there is only one orange, it is just that– an orange. If other oranges are added to the bowl, then it would be identified as the California orange, the ripe orange, the sweet orange, or the Seville orange.... It is through others that we clarify who we

---

[81] Benson, *op. cit.* pp. 15-22

are—and by extension who we want to be and who we don't want to be.

© Karen Sinclair

If there is only one orange, it is just that-- an orange. If other oranges are added to the bowl, then it would be identified as the California orange, the ripe orange, the sweet orange, the Seville orange...

Figure 5: Orange Context and Identity

That social architecture is almost entirely supported by relationships (often elusive), and is in that sense a conceptual entity crucially reliant on mind. Confusion arises when the individual, that unique and special combination of mind and body, fails to see their lot as a valid and worthwhile part of the architecture. In more tangible terms, it is when the seedless orange feels trapped by its seedlessness. The truth is: all people, just as they are, have worth. There is no bodily trap if we understand where the cultural doors are and how individual self worth, love and hatred develop. To use an analogy, the fact that there are oranges with seeds does not undermine the validity of seedless oranges. So too is each manifestation of humans, however alike or different from another.

As Professor Benson found in the study of the Tibetan monks we looked at earlier, *the human mind is not the servant of human biology.* In other words, a bodily circumstance does not *create* a mind's satisfaction or dissatisfaction about it (the circumstance). The circumstance just *is.* The satisfaction or dissatisfaction has some other source. Closer to home than the Tibetan monks is paralyzed football player Eric LeGrand[82]. He hurt himself during a game in New Jersey in 2010, but maintained an accepting approach about his new circumstances and his body. Knowledge that it is not the body that *creates* misery or joy has implications in attempts to fuse body and mind and the search for symmetry in mind and body. We may not be as mentally developed as the Tibetan monks, but we do have the capacity to act with intelligence and master our situations.

In a nutshell, there is a dilemma in the attempt to master the social environment—we *are* part of the fabric of that environment. We are not just *in* it. We inherit it, imitate behaviors, process and internalize values and leak our own contributions back into the social fabric. In this way our mind is fed by, is a component of, and leaves an imprint on

---

[82] Politi, Steve, Paralyzed Rutgers football player Eric LeGrand still has something to smile about www.nj.com, April 26, 2011

the environment. From this we can reason that its role in sexuality is interactive with the environment. This understanding advances the discussion providing further clarification that sexual identity and orientation are not only live attributes of an individual, dependent on biology and spirit, nurturing, intelligence and extelligence, but also in turn leaves its imprint so that each individual's sexual identity touches others in the environment.

Clearly however, mind, body and society only partially define who we are. Despite any power and state of mind, sexuality is reflected in activity. This study will now examine some of the factors that may trigger sexual activity.

CHAPTER 9: THE TURF OF SEXUAL ACTIVITY

...opposing factors ranging from desire to trauma at the extremes can affect particular observed behaviors... which may therefore be insufficient for conclusions about sexual orientation.

Similar to assertions in other parts of this discussion, genes, hormones, DNA and other biological markers may also have some role to play in sexual activity. They are however not the subject of this discussion. This discussion will attempt to isolate socio-psychological triggers of sexual activity.

Desire

As children grow into adulthood, sexual desire comes from within. Innate sexual urges begin to yearn for some satiety. Young adults begin to feel differently about themselves. More than likely this is innate. Think of it like a tingling from within, without direct external stimulus. Compare it with the state of being hungry. When someone who is hungry seeks to satisfy that hunger, their options are based on what is available, convenient, and what their upbringing has led them to consider as acceptable food. So what does a young adult do about his or her sexual urges? Boys experience unconscious events during sleep. Since it is unconscious and triggered during sleep, it seems safe to conclude that it occurs independently of the circumstances, the environment and in particular, independently of other individuals, male, female or other identity. As an unconscious event during sleep, one can also regard these early sexual awakenings to be independent of sexual orientation.

Having occurred, what then becomes of these early awakenings of desire in the conscious individual? Beyond sleep, all sexes more than likely may first move toward some accessible, convenient solution they consider acceptable in an attempt to satisfy desire. I would venture that the individual's hands and fingers may be among top choices initially, out of convenience. Later, as the individual matures, gains confidence or explores further, more options become convenient and accessible. In addition to that, what is considered acceptable can be expected to change over time, with age and in response to other dynamics.

The point of this illustration is that desire and its expression can be seen as two separate but related processes. Desire may or may not be triggered by external stimulation. Its origins may initially be unconscious and unrelated to identity and orientation.

Love

The ability to love is common in humans. That is, unless it gets foiled by experience. Indeed, the inability to love is regarded as a symptom of some psychosis. Love is a feeling of caring directed toward a person (or some thing). Its starting point is intrinsic. The recipient of love is the object, not the cause. We love because of who we are. As we saw in the section 'Internet Dating—Revealing the Sexual Intellect', Internet relationships may be used to demonstrate this since individuals interacting from separate global points remove the potential for responses by the senses and the unconscious transmission of chemical or other subconscious stimuli. The Internet creates a non chemical vacuum for interaction that may be used to illustrate how we can fall for illusions or deceptions presented to us. The virtual image is as unreal as a toy car or a toy animal that looks like the real thing. For example, a real-looking rubber snake thrown onto the ground is likely to elicit the same response as the real thing. The emotion comes from us, not from the snake. Our response is based on what we know and think about the snake. As truly as we can imagine ourselves on vacation by looking at Internet presentations of a vacation spot, we can imagine ourselves loving someone by connecting with them on the Internet. Neither, however, is stimulated by chemical or sensual reality. It is *virtual* reality. We can get excited about famous artist Michael Jackson live, repeatedly on the Internet. Yet, he remains dead. Rubber, virtual or real, the source of emotion is the same. It is your hearing and sight that receive input and collaborate with your brain to develop the emotions you feel. Love that a person feels does not come *from* someone else. Human responses are individual, filtered through the undefined interplay of intellect, education, values and a myriad of factors.

That process determines whether as individuals we would or would not love our neighbor's spouse, a kid, a sibling, someone of the same sex, someone of the opposite sex, or an assigned husband/ wife in an arranged union. Individual emotions are guided and shaped by that information and those values the individual subscribes to, eliminating and refining the selection of objects of our emotion. We turn away from those we consider inappropriate. These choices are more obvious in Internet dating where individuals consciously define filters and use them to screen out those with whom they do not want to communicate. The process is more subtle in active social situations, but the ability to love is still the same. Source and object of love are distinct and the process occurs in the source. Passive or active, the other person is only an object in the process and neither controls nor determines the process. What this means is that we have the capacity to love anyone we permit ourselves to. This knowledge can have an impact on how the individual perceives identity and orientation.

Although this discussion separates source, object and process, it is recognized that the love object need not be entirely uninvolved and may influence the process of love. People may do things or become or pretend or assume attitudes and postures to make others love them. This does not discount chemical and other reactions, but clearly, *you can't make someone love you.* Even in those situations, love can only occur if the source is responsive to that influence. Your love then, is not about another person, it is about You.

Availability

The 2010 census of the American population shows that for every age group, there is a greater population of females than males. If homosocializing was caused by an imbalance in population, one would expect differences in homosocializing among males and females to reflect this imbalance. Then, if homosocializing is related to homosexuality, then one can expect a preponderance of female homosexuality as females make do with each other, and no male homosexuality as the men select from the glut of females. Similarly, if that were the case, one would expect evidence of male polygamy as a natural result of the 'glut' in the female population. The evidence of both male and female homosexuals nullifies the argument that mere availability or unavailability of people of a particular gender can promote sexual orientation. Informal observation reveals both male homosocializing and female homosocializing. Popular media also document both male and female homosexual unions. One is inclined to conclude that availability may affect socializing but is not the determinant of sexual activity.

If we are blessed with the ability to love and have some inner desire, what then are the factors that convert this inner capability into a sexual action? There are many factors ranging from extremes of conscious behaviors to more subtle forms of persuasion and influence. I will briefly review some of these.

Conscious Choice

What occurs beyond desire depends on the overlap between what is convenient and accessible and what learning, exposure, education and knowledge find appropriate. Just as a hungry person whose upbringing socializes them as a vegetarian would first consider different food options from someone who is omnivorous, our values and what is acceptable and our understanding of the options available also play a role in what happens next. It influences the first steps a young adult takes as he or she moves beyond his or her own body to satisfy him or herself. It also influences the steps a mature adult makes in the quest to quench this inner spring. This is demonstrated in the previous discussion on tearoom encounters and Mark Thompson's documentation of habits of convenience and impersonal sexual encounters[83].

Force and persuasion

Predators may also affect an individual's determination of self. In that sense, force, persuasion and other forms of domination take advantage of a vulnerable situation and may sow seeds of vulnerability in an individual. In her book *Trauma and Recovery*[xxvii], Dr. Judith Herman explained how the effects of psychological trauma overwhelm the individual. Dr. Herman observed effects of trauma persisting even with no memory of the traumatic event. These traumatic effects include the opposite extremes of

---

[83] Thompson, Mark, *op. cit.* p. 43

repetition compulsion and complete dissociation. Early sexual exposure can in that way play a role in shaping the early activity and hence directing the later sexual habits and orientation of individuals. Dr. Herman's findings support the conclusions of this analysis that abuse may affect sexual behavior in unknown ways, including repeated attempts to relive the trauma, or compulsion to avoid a traumatic experience or relationship altogether. Whether the tendencies mirror or are in opposition to the experience is not at issue here, although contrasting experiences such as extreme aversion and depraved indulgence may result. The point of this discussion is that the experience does leave a sexual imprint. Like other forms of violence, the experience may lead to symptoms of trauma and an association of sexual experience with trauma. This is a social imprint in that it results from an act/s of violence.

Since tendencies and habits may take on the characteristics of preference, Dr. Herman's discussion illustrates then that adult sexual preferences characterized as sexual orientation can possibly be an individual's way of handling traumatic childhood experiences. So too, an individual can embrace, reject or adopt a particular sexual identity as a way of handling a traumatic experience.

Habit

Regularly repeated behavior is observed as a habit. The observation is no indicator of cause for the repetition. As previously discussed, opposing factors ranging from desire to trauma at the extremes can affect particular observed

behaviors.   It   follows   then   that   recognition   or
acknowledgement of a habit is not a factor on which to base
conclusions about sexual orientation. Although the behavior
may be consistent with a particular sexual orientation, the
orientation need not be the cause. For example, repeated
pleasure creates the psychological expectation of pleasure.
Subsequently, the expectation inspires repetition, in an
endless cycle. Simply put, all that statement is asserting is
that we look for pleasure in places where, and from people
from whom we have received it in the past. Individuals go
back to the same people/ same kind of people exploring
pleasure   repeatedly.   In   this   way,   our   socialization
(experience) helps shape our habits, as well as what we want,
what is important to us and how we see ourselves.

The point is that, although we start out with sexual urges—
(some innate function of our nervous system), our actions to
satisfy those urges are a mix of what is convenient, our
experience, what is presented to us, accustomed behavior,
and what we accept as appropriate. The Mark Thompson
cases of tearoom sex previously cited are perfect examples
of situations that allow individuals to gain sexual release by
impersonal contact devoid of aesthetic attraction and
emotion. One can see how such contact, repeated over time
becomes habit.

In common with many situations of habit, the partners we
choose, male or female, fat or muscular, innocent or
experienced can become preferences and our accustomed
way of operating. But habit is just one dimension among
many influences on our sexual practices and the way we
define ourselves sexually. Care must be taken in basing
conclusions about sexual identity and orientation on

acknowledged habit. It must also be taken into account in distinguishing between behaviors impelled by routine habits of convenience and behaviors characterized by pull factors such as attraction.

Physical Attraction

Physical attraction is a different 'kettle of fish'. Often visual, it is a function of what we see and in a western world where much of that is clothing and makeup, it can easily be slotted as social conditioning; it appeals to the aesthetic. From century to century what is physically attractive has changed with fashion. Whether it was voluptuous Victorian aesthetic or the thin Twiggy of the seventies, hips and lips, size and styles, subtle or psychedelic, they have defined a changeable aesthetic of attraction.

From Victorian outlandish costumes to today's almost naked revelations, the visual has been predominant in leading sexual attraction. That image is not static. Along with the changes across cultures, the evolution of the popular image suggests that image, including sexual image, is partly based on social conditioning. This means that our culture defines standards for us including standards of what is considered attractive. We respond in kind appreciating ourselves and others based on closeness to the popular ideal. Persuading ourselves that beauty is as thin as Twiggy in the 1960's, as voluptuous as Marilyn Monroe in the fifties, or as svelte as Tyra Banks in the early 2000s, is evidence that standards of beauty are culturally defined, and by extension, that physical attraction is a socio-cultural contrivance. As another example, perspectives of attractiveness over the years have included images as smooth as Cary Grant in the 40s, in contrast to muscular Arnold Schwarzneggar in the seventies, and as imperious as Sean Coombs in the early 2000s. Without evidence of some mass shift in human psyche, these dramatic shifts in standards may be regarded as socio-cultural. On the sexual front we need to look not at some inexplicable biology, but at the social imprint external to ourselves, a collective mediate experience,[84] to understand our attraction to a particular ideal. These are examples of physical attraction's essential *social* dimension and its dependence on contemporary aesthetics. The discussion does not imply that attraction is entirely a social phenomenon.

Stimulation– sensual

Stimulation on the other hand is a *physical* process or condition. The result may be described as excitement, alertness or awakening. The stimulus itself need not be physical. In contrast, attraction refers to our minds' interpretation of something external, while stimulation refers to our body's response. Where attraction is a state of mind, stimulation is more a condition of the body. We can say we are stimulated when we identify some response in our bodies. Stimulation is bodily active while attraction as described above can remain passive, although it too can create a state of stimulation.

---

[84] Sullivan, Harry Stack, *op. cit.*

In this discussion, sensual stimulation refers to the bodily response to provocation perceived by the senses. This includes the bodily response to what we smell, see, hear and think. This definition is inclusive of provocations from art, literature as well as realities in our presence. It however excludes discussion of the sense of touch which is handled separately in the later discussion.

For purposes of this writing, it is important to examine the cause and sources of that stimulation rather than to describe the transformations that occur during stimulation. In examining sensual stimulation, there are clear elements of social conditioning and the influence of past experiences. For example, as previously illustrated, we may receive stimulation from images of beauty which vary across societies and over time. Further, Deutsch and Krauss in their discussion of human responses, in their book *Theories of Social Psychology*[xxviii], concluded that among other things, a given response can be influenced by the reward associated with prior performances and the amount of work involved[85]. Concepts of "work" and "reward" are social perceptions relevant to the discussion of the imprint society has on human sexuality. Their presence demonstrates that responses are not automatic, but conditional. Sensual stimulation viewed from this angle therefore has the character of attraction in motion. It is a complex conditioned and conditional response to influences that do not on their own conjure meaning other than that attached by our social conditioning, knowledge, experience and education.

---

[85] Deutsch, Herman & Krauss, Robert M., Theories in Social Psychology, Basic Books Inc., NY, 1965, p.82

Even stronger evidence of the social imprint is the absence of consistency in gender response to stimuli. Responses do not change if gender is obscured. For example, with eyes closed, a particular scented perfume would create the same reaction in a subject if offered by a man or a woman. It is sexual alright; it can cause a sexual reaction. But it is not gender inspired. We hear a loud sound and it can make us afraid and anxious. We see a gun pointed at us and respond with fear. This is based on our knowledge and experience. We read a scary story and our hearts begin to pound in fear. This reflects our intellectual interpretation and understanding of the situation. The same intellectual, experiential and knowledge responses are true for placating sounds, appealing images and titillating stories. Our bodies are stimulated sensually one way or another based on what we know and understand. Popular evidence of this rests in the use of placebos. The placebo effect occurs when a medicine with no inherent benefit is administered to a patient who, believing that the medicine offers particular benefits, experiences those benefits. This is evidence that human bodily experiences can be knowledge based and supports the view that even stimulation can be knowledge based and therefore socio-culturally inspired.

Stimulation–physical

Like sensual and knowledge based stimulation, physical stimulation is a different dimension that triggers a physical response. As we see from reports of experiences of victims of predators, stimulation can occur by physical contact even in the presence of fear, doubt, unwillingness and uncertainty. Parts of the human body, whether it is the nervous system, the genes, hormones, etc. (which are a black box to this study) can respond to direct physical stimuli <u>without </u>knowledge, understanding or intellectual co-operation.

History has shown that people often use implements to accomplish physical sexual stimulation. Couples of both heterosexual and homosexual persuasion use asexual devises to stimulate each other. It is no mystery that physical stimulation can be accomplished even by mechanical devices, and is therefore independent of the gender of the stimulant. This supports the position that physical stimulation is not controlled by gender.

The reality is that people who avow homosexuality may nevertheless seek and respond to physical stimulation that is essentially heterosexual, and vice versa; people who avow heterosexuality may respond to physical stimulation that is essentially homosexual. One is led to conclude that neither the successful dispensation nor the successful receipt of physical stimulation is gender restricted. Again, Thompson's tearoom sex cases serve as another demonstration of physical release accomplished without emotion, specific orientation or affection. The conclusion from this is that the urge to be stimulated arises from within or is inspired by imperceptible sources; judgments however, about whether different kinds of physical stimulation are inspired by orientation, either heterosexual or homosexual, are flawed.

Stimulation– Drugs

Both legal and illegal drugs are also used to produce sexual stimulation. Some of these drugs work regardless of the presence of any other person or any conscious thought, creating chemical reactions equivalent to sexual pleasures. In fact, date rape drugs are credited with rendering individuals *unconscious* but *responsive*. Drugs prescribed to combat male impotence also produce physical effects equated with sexual arousal, for example by stimulating an increase in blood flow to sexual organs.[86] This influences the conclusion that sexual stimulation and sexual activity function independently of what we familiarly call sexual orientation. Sexual arousal is independent of sexual orientation and can occur regardless of inclination, thought or external influence. This suggests that our biology is not necessarily the driver of our sexual relationships and partnerships. The effect that drugs have on our bodies demonstrates that identity and orientation are not prerequisites to sexual functioning.

One is therefore inclined to conclude that particular conditions for sexual unions are then conscious or unconscious choices, not physical demands. Physical demands do not set pre-conditions about gender or other criteria. If criteria are present, they must arise from some other conscious or unconscious need. Consciously, we know we are choosing from various options. Unconsciously, we are unaware of the social exposure that is making one path seem more compelling to us than some other path. Either

---

[86] "How does Viagra work", www.viagra.com

way, we are not hapless servants of some sovereign, indomitable sexual orientation.

What value is this understanding? For people who want to live informed lives, this understanding could help to break through doubts, choices, concerns about orientation or habit. People seek pleasure in relationships. Understanding that orientation is separate from pleasure also means that people can comfortably introduce considerations about their values in their sexual lives without being concerned about denying themselves the full benefits of human sexual pleasure.

Value is not universal. This discussion is another element in the vast pool of available information. The holders of moral codes, for example churches, synagogues, mosques, have a role to play in shaping the moral fabric from an informed position. Understanding the information available to us, we can also develop perspectives and positions including moral wisdom, which are based on information and not on fear, misplaced sentiment and misinformation.

ABOUT WHOEVER

CHAPTER 10: HOW IT ALL COMES TOGETHER

Fusion of an interconnected mosaic

The ability to love and the capacity for love are common to both the male and female of our species. These individual abilities and capacities come together in a shared social, political and physical environment and share conceptual and material realities. Circumstances, influences and opportunities have an impact on those abilities and capacities and help shape how they develop and how we express and explore them. The Helen Boyd story[87] helps to highlight the distinction between who we are sexually and the opportunities we take to express ourselves. With comic insight, the fictional character Ziggy by Cartoonist Tom Wilson described this relationship between opportunity and expression in a manner that may be easier to comprehend: "Opportunity doesn't even need to knock if you just leave your door open to it!"

Consistent with this is the understanding that sexual arousal is verified by biological changes and can be caused by receiving sensual stimuli independently of the sexual biology

---

[87] Boyd, Helen, *op. cit.*

199

of any other person (i.e. people can be aroused independently of others). This means that if we pursue sexual arousal through sexual activity we are guided not by intrinsic homosexual or heterosexual biology, but by a moving platform of extrinsic circumstances; those that our five senses can respond to. In other words, the biology of arousal is *independent of* the gender of another person. Alternatively, if individuals base their sexual pursuits only on the biology of arousal, they may overlook influences from other dimensions and sidestep opportunities to make conscious decisions in particular circumstances.

By extension, if we identify ourselves based on our sexual preferences we are identifying ourselves not only by physical being, but also by elements of the same platform of external stimuli and circumstances that our senses respond to. In simple terms, we are not merely identifying who we are, but circumstances we prefer. Given the biology of arousal, and the truth that one does not have to be attracted to a dildo for it to work, it can be said that individuals: gay, straight, pansexual and omnisexual, do with their bodies whatever they (consciously or instinctively) deem acceptable whether it be with implements and tools or other persons of the same or opposite sex. In this context, doing is differentiated from being. Yet, in the development of the individual, doing ultimately shapes being and individuals are built by what they repeatedly do.

By superimposing itself over biology, cultural codes replace biology as the *operative* distinguishing features recognized by the sexes. In this way, sexuality masquerades in cultural codes and sociosexual symbols and can independently graft new varieties of costume without changing the human mannequin. As we socialize, it is these codes such as hair and dress and posture and not our biological capacities that help us to identify, and which influence our learning, attraction, attractiveness, habits and stimulation, and direct our love, affection and behavior. In this manner, every variety of sexual identity: gay, straight, intersex or other comes together as a designer meta-identity. There is fundamental commitment to this meta-identity and one can sometimes observe one of the partners in a same-gender union adopting the meta-identity of the absent gender.

Because of this sexual masquerade, the cultural imprint is therefore dominant in contemporary sexual relationships. Perceptions of people are filtered through culture. In this sense our preferences are socially acquired, and are just that, preferences. Sexual orientation is therefore not a life sentence, but more of a social composite that permeates our psyche. People in contemporary society can declare it, hide it, deny it, embrace it, and change it without in any way invalidating it.

We often assume that our actions are biologically induced because we are not aware of the social and environmental influences. Yet, both biology and the conditioning of culture or free choice have an imprint on individual identity. By extension, behaviors and orientations defined by *being,* as well as behaviors and orientations defined by *doings,* are integrated *in*divisibly into what we regard as the individual.

Over time, an array of different gender and identity markers has emerged. Despite the evident diversity, each form of identity in the array does not enjoy equal cultural acknowledgement and acceptance. It is customary to apply one of two gender identities at birth. There is general silence about intersexed and other births and census data show only two sexes. Additional identities arise through self-identification. Parents have also pronounced some sexual identity of a child even before the child displays sexual behaviors. There is no scientific consensus yet available.

Similarly there is no independent marker of sexual orientation. It is privately determined and varies in expression, denial and acknowledgement as documented in interviews conducted by Hamer and Copeland.[88] Though privately determined, factors, including rejection and trauma, may affect sexual orientation.[89]

The findings lead to a perspective of multifarious influences shaping sexual identity and orientation; Influences common to all, regardless of gender, expressed identity or orientation. Since no influence can be objectively identified in terms of extent, degree or dominance, all facets may be viewed together as a mosaic of interconnected influences.

---

[88] Hamer & Copeland, *op. cit.* p.64
[89] Hamer & Copeland, *op. cit.* p.65

SUMMARY

Although social imprints are the focus of *About Whoever: The social imprint on identity and orientation,* there are many elements. Facets of human sexuality may be represented as shown in the illustration in Appendix 3: Sexual Mosaic. They may be called a mosaic because they are dissimilar and relationships and connections between them are changeable and inconsistent. In reviewing the mosaic, it may be noted that all facets are not labeled. This is done because the discussion does not presume a comprehensive definition of the full constitution of human gender, sexual identity and orientation. It also does not pretend to fully grasp all dimensions of the social imprint on identity and orientation. The sexual mosaic is representative, and not a full depiction of all dimensions of human sexuality. Elements in the mosaic interact and exert influence in unspecified ways. The book is offered as part of the quest to understand humanity, and presents the sexual mosaic as a synthesis of signposts representing the dimension of sexuality.

In summary, many factors influence human sexuality, but the nature and effect of the influences are unpredictable. Gender has traditionally been equated with sex organs but that perspective is not contemporary. Babies are given gender labels at birth, usually male or female based on sex organs. Children are groomed, nurtured and educated based on this presumed dichotomous human gender but in contemporary society this may be challenged later in life. That natal gender assignment forms the universal kernel of identity. Traditionally, society has not made room for births, nurturing or development outside of this dichotomy and it has been the basis of traditional sexual identity.

Contemporary society however recognizes and acknowledges an array of gender descriptions and sexual identities, those arising either from traditional assumptions, as well as those derived through self identification. Where traditional identity was fixed, contemporary society confronts a changeable, dynamic or developmental concept of sexual identity. Individual sexual identity today may be directed by individual choice and preference and defined by many social processes. It is also sometimes aided by surgery. Although that is a contemporary perspective, these are turbulent times and opposing views constantly clash in impassioned debates supporting traditional and contemporary perspectives.

Many truths were summarized concerning gender, identity and orientation. Gender defines what the sex is, while sexual identity is an expression of who the person is sexually, and sexual orientation is defined by how an individual is inclined to relate to others sexually. They are all subject to imprints from social processes and forces. While neither sexual identity nor sexual orientation is purely dependent on society, it is difficult to distinguish between social, biological or other influences. It is also true that different identities and orientations whether heterosexual, homosexual or other, all thrive side by side under the same social and other influences, pressures, practices and laws making it impossible to identify specific roots of any. There is no dispute that there were originally only two genders, masculine and feminine, but it is also true that today an extended variety of gender realities, sexual identities and orientations manifest themselves in contemporary society.

In Chapter 2: Sociosexual Identity, it was recognized that contact in social circumstances is filtered through many pseudo-sexual accoutrements. In that section, the analysis revealed differences between identity and behavior and between *socio*sexual, homosexual and homo*social* behaviors. Examination of homosocial activity uncovered a positive role in heterosexual development.

Chapter 3: Anatomy and Identity looked at physical traits we typically use to characterize masculinity and femininity. Biology, including genes and hormones, subtleties of voice and muscle and human intervention has a significant though only partial role in cultivating the anatomy we associate with gender identity.

The human environment was reviewed broadly in three sections: Chapter 4: The Social Sentence of the Sexes, Chapter 6: Law, Policy and Rights, and Chapter 7: Social Convention and Practices. These explored ways that some aspects of our environment confine, expand or proscribe our sexual agenda. With reference to specific changes in the environment, changes in values and a new morality are revealed.

Examination of the involvement of intellect in shaping perspectives, choices and behavior in Chapter 5: The Sentence as Intellectual Activity, highlighted the role of self in expression of identity and revealed human sexual intellect. Evidence of technical and industrial change during the industrial and technological revolutions not only documents change, but is also evidence of man's intrinsic and social capacities, seen echoed in his sexual pursuits.

Sexual and sociosexual understanding are examined in a broader human context in Chapter 8: Beyond Sexual Horizons. Whoever we are, identity has no reality except within the context of other people. This section also extended the understanding of sexual intellect into concepts of *being* gay or straight and *doing* gay or straight and led to the discussion in Chapter 9: The Turf of Sexual Activity, of the distinction between sexual doings (activities) and sexual identity and orientation. It showed that love, desire, stimulation, and drugs, among other things can spur sexual action and that sexual activity and satisfaction are not restricted by gender. Collating the various insights one may define a contemporary human sexual mosaic.

CONCLUSIONS

Sexual identity and sexual orientation include a mosaic of interacting and interdependent factors about which not everything is known. Some observations are natal while evidence of others emerges in maturity and at other stages in human development. Influences are not static but grow and develop over time, a whole integrated being, the adult human. There are many layers to that identity of which biology is only one. The social imprint reflects another. How the adult human is constituted, how he acts, what is required of him, how he is perceived and how he feels are all dimensions of that identity. Today is witness to the dawn of a new age. It reflects the cumulative intellectual, experiential and interactive behaviors of humans over the years since the beginning of original man and original woman. Identity today is a dynamic of *being*.

Through the discussion of sociosexual identity, it is clear that the human being is not merely gregarious in behavior, but also in his *constitution*, in who he is and how he matures. He develops partly by social processes. An individual does not need identity to exist, but to socialize, interact with and function in context of other human beings. There is no concept of identity without the context of society. Although individuals *need* no identity to exist, they *have* no identity without the presence of others. Existence without identity is inconceivable. In this sense, sexual identity is not a survival or existential need, but a social requirement, aligned with healthy development.

Gender declarations at birth are one dimensional in that they are based only on the observation of genitals. Like sexual identity, persons do not need gender declarations to exist, but to participate in modern life. Gender declarations are sometimes 'normalized' to suit social expectations. Modern lifestyle is a complex social phenomenon and there is a symbiotic relationship between the individual and society. People collectively develop society, define lifestyles and aspects of humanity and are simultaneously developed and changed by society. One of those aspects is sexual identity, declared at birth and developed, nurtured and educated in an increasingly complex society.

Human biology, though tangible and more easily discernable is no more or no less vital and important in defining who an individual is, than is society. The basis of gender declarations at birth, sexual organs are not determinants of sexual identity and sexual orientation in adults, neither are genes, biology and DNA, although they are all relevant. Instead, adult relationships have multifarious dimensions. Biology does not fall in love and have relationships, people do... whole, multi-dimensional folks. Since people can take intelligent action and are not servants of human biology, declarations at birth are inadequate to contain and constrain paths to adulthood.

Human biology, however, does have a role in pleasure and can therefore not be ignored in the attempt to understand the role of gender in the pursuit of adult relationships. Pleasure is one of the motivators of that pursuit. Physical pleasure results from physical, emotional and other stimulation. From the discussion in Chapter 9: The Turf of Sexual Activity, we can conclude that physical stimulation of humans is not conditioned by the gender of either the giver or receiver. Sexual identity and orientation are therefore not prerequisites to sexual functioning and sexual pleasure.

Although society has progressed with a heterosexual dominant reality based historically on observable duality in gender biology, the rainbow array of sexual profiles in contemporary society cannot be denied. As discussed, sexual development whether homosexual or heterosexual is a process that occurs through social interactions that nourish individuals. However, while that nourishing is indeterminate, individual behavior is self determining. This suggests that behavior and conscious action determine lifestyles, despite genetics.

The variety of sexual identities may be a procedural outcome of dynamic, progressive social processes, beginning with the original two sexual identities, male and female. Progressively curious behavior is not inhibited by static biology. This supports the perspective that from two sexes with a single heterosexual relationship with each other, contemporary society's network of orientations may be the outcrop representing human inclination to probe and uncover additional relationships and frontiers. Similar to the snowball effect of the industrial revolution, human sexuality today may be regarded as a reflection of the dynamic of increased awareness of alternative lifestyles.

How or why individual character and dimension emerge is irrelevant to the validity of the existence of any sexual identity or orientation. Validity is not a facet of right or wrong, law or flaw but of reality and truth of existence. This means that whether people are born that way or their upbringing or circumstances or other factors come into play in their sexual development, does not change their reality.

Gart T. Marx in the introductory essay to his book *Muckraking Sociology: Research as Social Criticism*[xxix] presents important ideas that reflect the social responsibilities of analysts. I share his view of the importance of *intent* and integrity of purpose. In considering this analysis, I believe that in some areas it is adequate that I merely present the ideas. For example, in recognizing the various influences on identity and its subjectivity, and the factors that we as a society use to recognize and acknowledge the different sexes. However I feel a social responsibility to make a few proposals with regard to some aspects of this analysis.

Firstly, there are areas where the common knowledge is inadequate. I advocate further research into and steps that lead to greater and greater understanding and recognition of ourselves and to the dissemination of this information to ordinary folk. One key concern is that understanding self should be part of general curricula not merely the privy of researchers, anthropologists and psychologists, to trickle down from where they are and be disseminated through psychological treatment programs and therapies. Instead, basic information should become part of our general knowledge, a requirement like math or language. This should enable individuals to flourish with understanding as they develop and better equip parents and social institutions in conducting their responsibilities. In particular, statistical information on births other than male and female needs to be collected. Documenting only male and female births perpetuates the historic perspectives, promotes 'normalization' and ostracizes the intersex population. Census taking needs to be inclusive.

I see the main areas for further work initially to be those mentioned in chapters 4 and 5 of this book. Hopefully, as the body of knowledge, information and understanding expands, these areas will also change and grow as we use new information as stepping stones toward understanding. We need to proceed with compassion, inclusiveness and understanding.

Specifically, the needed areas for research and mass dissemination of findings of research are the areas of education of the mind, education and development of the human spirit, influences on human sexuality, and human survival as a species. In particular, people can benefit from education about the distinctions between who they are, the society and their roles in it, and their biology. It is socially responsible not only to disseminate important information, but to find ways to integrate it into our cultural practices.

It is important to recognize the need for new vocabulary as we progress. This is not a small thing. Vocabulary is one method to succinctly express a single body of information with a mutual understanding. Once we discover a new idea, explain it and attach a label to it, that label can be substituted in every forum for the details of the understood idea. New vocabulary represents progress. As in this book, one does not have to agree with the concepts of homosocializing, sociosexual identity and the culture of straights, in order to understand them. These expressions may be used to represent the entire discussions that defined them in this book. I envision hope for movement toward greater understanding within our generation, if not within my lifetime.

The analysis suggests that neither heterosexual behaviors nor homosexual behaviors are any more natural universally than is placing value on telling the truth, placing value on martyrdom, placing value on suicide missions, placing value on life. By this yardstick, cultural practices sustained by a group are those values and belief systems adhered to by the majority of that group. While it is acceptable to have cultural practices, is there a divine right to persecute any minority? I think not.

Formal regulators of human value systems, (religious and other institutions), may benefit from the perspective that there may be both people who *are* gay or straight and those who *do* gay or straight. Like a parent who learns new skills to care for a child with needs different from theirs, these institutions may benefit from understanding the populace in their care. While I would not advocate that any institution should *change* its value systems, I do believe that perceiving who man is and how he is constituted, could bring light to their paths and values. Behavioral prescriptions may be affected. In addition, regulators of value systems may benefit from the perspective that the human mind is not servant to the human body. Conclusions surrounding *why* heterosexuality or homosexuality may be wrong or right could be aided by the understanding of the social sentence of the sexes and discussions about the impact of human survival, education, religion on our value systems. Reasons for our values may be lost over time, but the values linger still.

Parents, and those holding responsibility for the lives of others, may benefit from the distinctions between homosocial and other behaviors and the discussion about sociosexual elements. They may be encouraged to withhold judgments concerning a child based on their preferences in clothing, whether or not they like the way their genitals look or are satisfied with their noses, genitals or hair they are given. Genes don't love, people do. The whole individual, not any one gene, is the final determinant of expression of identity. Parents feeling responsibility for the sexuality of their children may find the concept of the budding rose bush helpful, both for their own enlightenment and for their children's. Feelings of guilt may be tutored by understanding the sexual intellect, the contrast with the turf of sexual activity, and those implications beyond the sexual horizons which are analyzed in this book. Understanding the concept of sexual intellect may be important to understanding the internet generation and perspectives about relationships and bonding that may differ from traditional ones.

Similarly, understanding gio indexes may help individuals separate their yearnings to play roles of peter pan or the fairy or scrooge, from their gender, identity and orientation. Along with the understanding of the unbounded human capacity to love, the role of intellect, and value in seeking and pursuing pleasure discussed in this book, the gio indexes may help people see more clearly in the mirror. In addition, the gio indexes could be a pit stop on the road to full understating as individuals contribute to the further development and clarification of gio relationships and dimensions.

Culture is also not the final authority on the sanctity of *being.* It is therefore inappropriate for the dominant majority, whatever it is, to presume to reflect perfect understanding of the varieties of being and characteristics of perfection. Concepts of 'Right' and 'wrong' are not equivalent to 'majority' and 'minority' populations.

The body of research on human sexuality may benefit from the perceptions in this book of sexuality as both *being* and *doing.* Recalling the vivid example of one-legged men in a sample population, scientists taking a fresh look at previous research may examine how self-identification and sample populations used may have affected inconclusive findings. The search for the gay gene or the straight gene or any genetic and DNA analysis may also be aided by understanding the sociosexual mosaic of elements of human sexuality and its connotation that not everyone is born gay or straight, and by understanding the rose bush principle.

These perceptions have implications for leaders and decision makers. Whoever they are, leaders should recognize that they represent only *one* example of the spectrum of human possibility. The leader of a democracy needs to be able to lead the entire spectrum of humans within the scope of the relevant geography. That person needs to be able to view his or her charge, not from his or her own perspective alone, but from an objective position that takes others into account. While leaders do share responsibility for moral direction and cultural perceptions of right and wrong, they also have responsibility for understanding beliefs, values and information and respecting them all. Understanding is key. It is not satisfactory to be swayed by the loudest or the most popular view.

Lastly, and most importantly violence and hate are associated with sexual orientation and identity in contemporary society. The perception of different identities and orientations as different expressions of the same origins and influences, should offer a shared foundation for approaching each other in peace, despite displays of difference. I may not have gotten it all right, but I do hope that at least some of the ideas and analyses in this book will be of value to someone. While we know that we perceive tangibles, expressions and behaviors, we all perceive them imperfectly.

Karen Sinclair

APPENDIX 1: GENDER, IDENTITY AND ORIENTATION INDEX TABLES

Table 1: Original Gio Index

Table 2: Historical Gio Index

Table 3: Contemporary Gio Index

Table 4: Contemporary Transgender Gio Index

Table 5: Contemporary Transex Gio Index

Table 6: Contemporary Orientation- Based Gio Index.

Table 7: Contemporary Transvestite Gio Index

APPENDIX 2: LIST OF ILLUSTRATIONS

Figure 1: Rose Bush Perspectives
Figure 2: One Legged Research Principle
Figure 3: The Sociosexual Life Sentence
Figure 4: The Ice Cream Principle
Figure 5: Orange Context and Identity

ABOUT WHOEVER

APPENDIX 3: SEXUAL MOSAIC

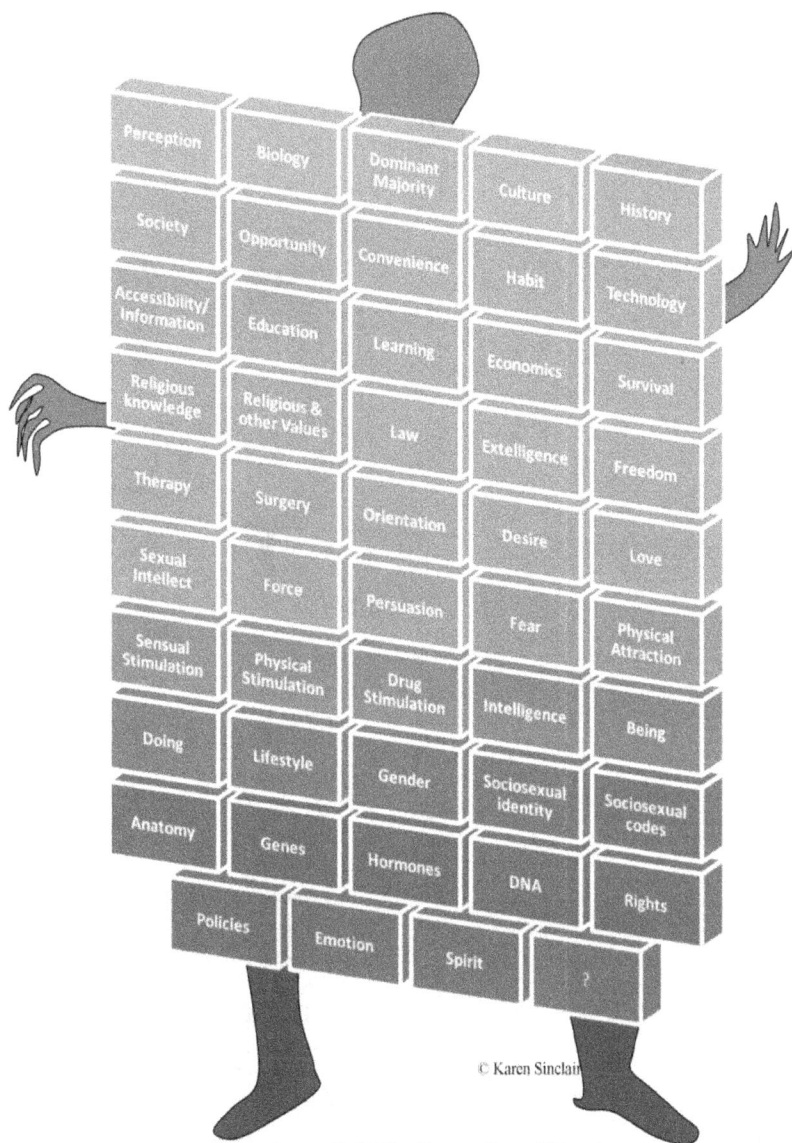

Appendix 3: The Human Sexual Mosaic

INDEX

acceptance, 3, 5, 6, 7, 12, 45, 49, 76, 118, 123, 133, 143, 173, 175, 201
availability, 187
beliefs, xii, 39, 76, 98, 104, 105, 117, 126, 130, 140, 142, 215
bisexual, 12, 13, 15, 158, 160, 165, 172, 175
civil union, 120, 121, 123, 124, 125
contextual identity, 15
cross dresser, 60, 149
culture of straights, 43, 61, 93, 123, 134, 146, 158, 164, 212
domestic partner, 120, 121, 123, 125, 126
domestic partnership, 120, 123, 124, 125
education, xviii, xx, 52, 53, 90, 92, 93, 95, 96, 97, 99, 100, 106, 133, 143, 168, 178, 186, 188, 193, 211, 213
extelligence, 24, 134, 135, 136, 137, 138, 139, 182
gay, xii, xxi, 5, 8, 12, 13, 34, 45, 53, 62, 67, 77, 78, 103, 116, 119, 120, 122, 123, 143, 158, 160, 164, 170, 171, 172, 173, 174, 175, 176, 178, 200, 201, 206, 212, 214
gender, xi, 3, 4, 5, 6, 7, 8, 10, 11, 13, 14, 15, 16, 18, 22, 23, 26, 27, 28, 29, 31, 33, 34, 36, 37, 38, 39, 40, 41, 42, 43, 45, 46, 47, 49, 50, 52, 53, 54, 56, 57, 58, 60, 61, 62, 64, 67, 71, 72, 73,

79, 81, 82, 83, 94, 98, 106, 109, 113, 115, 116, 130, 133, 134, 148, 149, 150, 151, 153, 154, 156, 157, 160, 162, 164, 171, 172, 187, 194, 195, 196, 200, 201, 202, 203, 204, 205, 206, 208, 209, 213
gender compulsion, 30, 39
gender hierarchy, 41, 43
gender identity, 7, 23, 31, 34, 43, 57, 64, 115, 156, 205
genes, 19, 33, 38, 46, 47, 48, 55, 59, 71, 77, 80, 155, 167, 175, 176, 183, 195, 205, 208
gio index, 11, 156, 157, 158, 161, 164, 165, 213
gio relationship, 156, 157, 159, 160, 162, 164, 165, 214
hermaphrodite, 3, 4, 6, 158
heterosexual, xii, 8, 11, 12, 13, 14, 15, 34, 60, 62, 84, 85, 86, 87, 89, 90, 91, 92, 103, 112, 114, 116, 121, 122, 123, 125, 133, 138, 143, 149, 152, 157, 158, 165, 171, 172, 173, 175, 178, 195, 200, 205, 209, 212
homosexual, xii, 8, 13, 15, 34, 35, 62, 86, 89, 114, 118, 119, 122, 152, 158, 171, 172, 174, 175, 187, 195, 200, 205, 209, 212
homosocial, 152, 154, 205, 213
homosocializing, 187, 212

identity, x, xi, xii, xiv, xv, 5, 7, 8, 10, 11, 13, 14, 15, 16, 19, 20, 21, 22, 23, 27, 30, 31, 33, 35, 37, 38, 39, 41, 42, 45, 46, 47, 49, 50, 51, 52, 53, 54, 55, 56, 57, 60, 61, 67, 71, 75, 77, 79, 96, 109, 113, 115, 116, 125, 130, 133, 135, 137, 139, 143, 147, 149, 151, 153, 154, 156, 157, 160, 162, 164, 165, 169, 170, 172, 179, 182, 184, 186, 196, 201, 202, 203, 204, 205, 206, 207, 208, 209, 210, 213, 215

intelligence, xii, 22, 103, 134, 137, 138, 140, 181, 182

intersex, 4, 5, 6, 10, 35, 37, 40, 47, 125, 158, 164, 201, 211

intersexual, 9, 10, 14, 114

kaleidoscope, 11, 43, 46, 47, 59, 67, 155

language, xvii, 25, 29, 30, 34, 39, 40, 41, 50, 72, 93, 95, 178, 211

law, xiii, xviii, 91, 92, 117, 118, 120, 121, 122, 123, 125, 126, 140, 141, 142, 176, 210

learning, 52, 92, 93, 95, 96, 97, 99, 111, 143, 144, 170, 174, 177, 188, 201

lesbian, 8, 12, 13, 34, 158, 160, 171, 172

lifestyle, xiii, 45, 162, 170, 172, 173, 174, 208

marriage, xi, xiii, 19, 85, 92, 103, 120, 121, 122, 123, 125, 126, 141

masquerade, 42, 50, 201

new morality, 139, 141, 142, 206

orientation, ix, x, xi, xii, xiv, xv, 5, 8, 11, 13, 14, 15, 16, 22, 23, 34, 35, 45, 52, 53, 60, 64, 77, 79, 90, 96, 106, 113, 116, 126, 130, 134, 135, 139, 143, 146, 151, 153, 154, 155, 156, 157, 158, 160, 162, 164, 165, 168, 169, 170, 172, 175, 178, 182, 184, 186, 189, 190, 195, 196, 197, 201, 202, 203, 204, 206, 209, 210, 213

pseudosocial, 10

rainbow, xx, 13, 209

religion, 98, 103, 104, 105, 106, 213

religious, 12, 25, 85, 89, 98, 100, 101, 104, 105, 106, 122, 142, 144, 145, 146, 148, 154, 212

rose bush, 4, 5, 7, 8, 13, 34, 47, 88, 213, 214

rose bush principle, 88, 214

same gender loving, 13, 34, 158

sentence, 38, 75, 83, 95, 109, 113, 114, 115, 122, 176, 201, 213

sexual hierarchy, 44

sexual identity, ix, xviii, xix, 7, 8, 10, 11, 12, 14, 15, 23, 27, 33, 34, 35, 38, 39, 41, 42, 43, 45, 46, 47, 50, 51, 52, 54, 55, 56, 58, 60, 62, 67, 72, 77, 79, 106, 109, 116, 125, 133, 137, 139, 143, 150, 151, 154, 157, 158, 165, 168, 170, 178, 182, 189, 190, 201, 202, 203, 204, 206, 208, 210

sexual intellect, 111, 206, 213

sexual mosaic, 203, 206

sexual orientation, xiv, xviii, xix, 8, 13, 14, 15, 16, 126, 133, 145, 146, 151, 153, 154, 155, 156, 157, 158, 172, 175, 183, 184, 187, 189, 190, 196, 197, 202, 204, 207, 208, 215

SGL, 8, 34, 59, 158, 160, 161

Sociosexual, 33, 37, 45, 50, 51, 56, 63, 66, 74, 86, 92, 168, 205, 217

sociosexual attraction, 66

sociosexual diplomacy, 30

sociosexual fusion, 85

sociosexual identity, 10, 38, 41, 48, 49, 51, 54, 57, 61, 67, 207, 212

straight, xx, 8, 12, 13, 143, 158, 160, 162, 170, 175, 178, 200, 201, 206, 212, 214

technology, xii, xviii, 11, 86, 111, 140, 144, 167, 177

transgender, 9, 10, 14, 56, 57, 60, 61, 125, 160, 161, 162, 164, 166

transsexual, 8, 10, 12, 14, 34, 40, 158, 162

transvestite, 54, 60, 165

221

BIBLIOGRAPHY

[i] Wright, William, Born That Way, Alfred A. Knopf, Inc., New York, 1998

[ii] Stoller, Robert, Sex and Gender: On the Development of Masculinity and Femininity, Science House, New York, 1968

[iii] Childe, Gordon, Man Makes Himself, The New American Library, New York, 1936

[iv] Wilson, Edward O., On Human Nature, Harvard University Press, Cambridge, 1978

[v] Dreger, Alice, PhD., Shifting the Paradigm of Intersex Treatment, for the Intersex Society of North America, http://www.intersexinitiative.org/pdf/dreger-compare.pdf , September 25, 2007

[vi] Rothman, Barbara Katz, Genetic Maps and Human Imaginations: The Limits of Science in Understanding Who We Are, W. W. Norman & Company Inc., New York, 1998.

[vii] Byrne, David, How Music Works, McSweeney's, San Francisco, 2012

[viii] Maccoby, Eleanor Emmons and Jacklin, Carol Nagy, The Psychology of Sex Differences, Stanford University Press, California, 1974

[ix] Stein, Ralph Michael, "A Sect Apart: A History of the Legal Troubles of the Shakers" (1981). Pace Law Faculty Publications. Paper 216. http://digitalcommons.pace.edu/lawfaculty/216

[x] Tainter, Joseph A. The Collapse of Complex Societies, Cambridge University Press, Cambridge, 1988

[xi] Stewart, Ian and Cohen, Jack, Figments of Reality, Cambridge University Press, Cambridge, 1997.

[xii] Pert, Candace B., Molecules of Emotion: Why You Feel The Way You Feel, Scribner, New York, 1997.

[xiii] Castleman, Michael, Gallagher-Thompson, Dolores and Naythons, Matthew, There's Still a Person In There, G.P. Putnam's Sons, New York, 1999

[xiv] Selling, Joseph A. ed., Embracing Sexuality—Authority and experience in the Catholic Church, Ashgate Publishing Company, Hampshire, 2001

[xv] Smith, Janet E. Humanae Vitae: a generation later, The Catholic University of America Press, Washington, 1991

[xvi] Olson, Harriett Jane, ed., The Book of Discipline of the United Methodist Church, The United Methodist Publishing House, Tennessee, 1996

[xvii] Adler, Mortimer J., Intellect: Mind Over Matter, Macmillan Publishing Company, New York, 1990.

[xviii] Burrelli, D.F. (2012). The repeal of "Don't Ask, Don't Tell": Issues for Congress, Washington, D.C. Congressional Research Service

[xix] Sullivan, Harry Stack, M.D. The Fusion of Psychiatry and Social Science, with introduction and commentaries by Helen Swick Perry, W.W. Norton & Company, Inc., New York, 1964.

[xx] Hoffer, Eric, The True Believer, Thoughts on the Nature of Mass Movements, Harper & Row Publishers Inc., New York, 1951

[xxi] Parsons, Jacquelynne E., ed. The Psychobiology of Sex Differences and Sex Roles, Hemisphere Publishing Corporation, 1980

[xxii] Boyd, Helen, My Husband Betty- Love, Sex and Life with a Crossdresser, Thunder's Mouth Press, New York, 2003

[xxiii] Corning, Peter, Nature's Magic, Synergy in Evolution and the Fate of Humankind, Cambridge University Press, Cambridge, 2003

[xxiv] Benson, Herbert, M.D. and Proctor, William, Your Maximum Mind, Random House of Canada, Inc. Toronto, 1987

[xxv] Thompson, Mark, ed. Long Road to Freedom: The Advocate History of the Gay and Lesbian Movement, The Advocate, Los Angeles, 1994.

[xxvi] Hamer, Dean H. and Copeland, Peter, The Science of Desire: The Search for the Gay Gene and the Biology of Behavior, Simon & Schuster, New York, 1994.

[xxvii] Herman, Judith L., Trauma and Recovery, Basic Books, 1997

[xxviii] Deutsch, Morton and Krauss, Robert M, Theories in Social Psychology, Basic Books Inc., 1965

[xxix] Marx, Gart T., Muckraking Sociology: Research as Social Criticism, Transaction Books, 1972

###

www.ingramcontent.com/pod-product-compliance
Lightning Source LLC
Chambersburg PA
CBHW062213270326
41930CB00009B/1725